Threading a Dream

A Poet on the Nile

John Greening

Gatehouse Press

Published in 2017 by
Gatehouse Press Limited
32 Grove Walk
Norwich NR1 2QG
www.gatehousepress.com

ISBN 978-0-9934748-7-3

About Gatehouse Press

Gatehouse Press is a small literary press based in Norwich. We produce poetry pamphlets, short fiction, and the award-winning journal *Lighthouse*, and our aim as a press is to give a platform to new writers. All staff are volunteers, and all profits go back into publishing. For more information, including how to submit work to *Lighthouse*, see our website: http://www.gatehousepress.com

Text set in Garamond and Day Roman. Used under licence.

Special thanks to Lee Seaman, James Higham and Rosie Greening.

Cover art and illustrations by Rosie Greening
Cover design by Lee Seaman
Printed and bound in the UK

For Jane,
with Alan Bolesworth and Stuart Evans

Poetry by John Greening

Westerners, 1982
Winter Journeys, 1984
The Tutankhamun Variations, 1991
Fotheringhay and Other Poems, 1995
The Coastal Path, 1996
The Bocase Stone, 1996
Nightflights, New & Selected Poems, 1998
Gascoigne's Egg, 2000
Omm Sety, 2001
The Home Key, 2003
Iceland Spar, 2008
Hunts: Poems 1979-2009, 2009
Knot, 2013
To the War Poets, 2013
Nebamun's Tomb, 2016
Heath (with Penelope Shuttle), 2016

Threading a Dream: a Poet on the Nile

Contents

Poems

It flows through old hush'd Egypt and its sands,
Like some grave mighty thought threading a dream

LEIGH HUNT

Remembering is for those who have forgotten.

PLOTINUS

Westerners

we ferried our past across here
our furniture   our favourite things
the familiar parts of our life

we reconstructed them to make
ourselves an opulent future
and barricade oblivion

you will recognise us among
these everlasting earth treasures
in a gold mask   or in black granite

in the clean slot of a hieroglyphic
though you thought we were dead and strange
you will recognise us   we are

still here   we are the westerners

Foreword: The Cataract

Anwar Sadat was assassinated on the very day that Jane and I moved into our council flat in Arbroath. We had only returned from Egypt a couple of months before, later than planned because I heard at the last minute that I had won First Prize at the Alexandria International Poetry Festival. We stayed on so I could receive it from the hands of President Sadat's wife, Jehan (a Shelley specialist) and read some of my poems to an invited audience on the site of the Pharos, one of the Seven Ancient Wonders of the World. We had our own tragic reasons for heading so suddenly to the other extremity of the Roman Empire, but I recall the fuzzy black-and-white images on our tiny portable TV as we carried our few possessions into the flat. Sadat was gunned down live on television by his own army officers on 6th October, 1981. As the headlines put it at the time: the Egyptians had killed their Pharaoh. Many others died, too, though Mrs Sadat survived and Hosni Mubarak, the vice-president, was only wounded. He took over later that month and at his inauguration the dead president's widow apparently advised him to 'grab hold of the country'. Thirty years later, as I sit down to write this memoir, the country has decided it's time to grab hold of President Hosni Mubarak. He is in prison, as are his sons, one of whom was being groomed to succeed him. It might have looked like the end of an era for the Egyptians when Mubarak took over, and perhaps once again when he was deposed, but in reality little ever changes in their country. Except, of course, the population. When we lived on the Nile there were 40 million people clustered along its narrow valley. That figure has now doubled.

Arriving in Northeast Scotland had marked our own shift from the Old to the Middle Kingdom. Ahead of us lay jobs and children, that long winding middle stretch with all its temples and tombs, but also a cataract known to all newly-hatched poets, the first collection. *Westerners* would appear eighteen months later, an all-Egyptian affair whose sand-dune yellow cover still occasionally winks – if not like the Pharos, then at least the Bell Rock Light – from the shelves of secondhand bookshops. Poetry was my New Kingdom and what follows in *Threading a Dream* is as much the story of the 'Growth of a Poet's Mind' (Wordsworth's subtitle to *The Prelude*) as it is an account of a young couple's life on the Upper Nile. For many years I tried to turn away from the Egyptian experience, feeling that I had dealt with it already and that it was too easy to write about the exotic. What was difficult was to write about your own back yard. My Huntingdonshire back yard has since been well and truly dug over, as have those beyond it, in New Jersey, Mannheim, Hounslow... they recede like hypostyle halls. Yes, it kept recurring: the imagery, the aesthetic even. Tutankhamun completely dominated my 1991 Bloodaxe collection. Omm Sety and Nebamun came along a few years later, and Akhenaten never left. Nor were there only poems, but also – as the following pages will reveal – plays, short stories, articles.

During the summer of 2011 I read several memoirs, including Andrew McNeillie's *An Aran Keening* and Roger Garfitt's *The Horseman's Word* (Roger had accepted some of my very earliest Egypt poems when he was editor of *Poetry Review* and was a constant source of encouragement to a young poet just setting out). It occurred to me that these prose accounts were about things that had happened to their authors as long ago as our own experiences in Upper Egypt. Surely they weren't beyond recall. Jane had kept a diary, after all. There were photographs, memorabilia, even an old cine film my father had taken. And I had a carrier bag full of our weekly letters rescued from my parents' house. A book began to take shape.

The best words in the best order have a curious power, as I am sure the priests of ancient Egypt knew: their *Book of the Dead* is full of spells and invocations for bringing about change. They recited aloud as a way of making connections between this world and other worlds, to unite the living and the dead, the past, present and future. 'I am Yesterday,' one of the lines runs, 'I know Today'. There will be readers who agree with W. H. Auden that 'poetry makes nothing happen' (today or tomorrow), but I am inclined to disagree. Poetry, and discovering that I really could write it, that it could capture some essential quality of the place, undoubtedly made Egypt happen for me. The telling of how it happened, nevertheless, does require the cooler guiding hand of narrative prose. So, rather as Auden and Louis MacNeice did in their *Letters from Iceland* (another desert country which would come to have great significance for me) I have interspersed some of my Egyptian poems throughout this memoir, selected from over thirty years' work – a few of them finding their way into a book for the first time. My younger daughter has also kindly provided a series of drawings to accompany them.

I had long been fascinated by what might be called (it's a landmark essay by William Golding) 'Egypt from My Inside' – the *idea* of Egypt: painted tombs and labyrinthine temples and animal gods, mythology and mysticism and ritual. But experiencing the place itself was an assault on the senses as well as on certain cherished Western values. It hit me like that wall of heat that met us as we stepped out of the plane in Cairo. It disorientated me, changed me for good, saving me from several aspects of myself: innate caution, for instance, a tendency either to romanticise, or to make everything cerebral, grittily intellectual. There was a sense of plunging into a new and risky element, something Ted Hughes had all but advised me to do in the letters he sent me before we left. He more than anyone understood the hidden, potentially dangerous powers a poet has access to. One of the recurrent metaphors in *Threading a Dream* (unsurprisingly, given Aswan's chief claim to fame) is that of the dam. I believe there are deep turbines whose extraordinary output we may never even notice, but poetry is capable of driving them. In Egypt I felt I was exposed to those forces, and I had no choice but to write. In many ways, *Westerners* composed itself. It is a book full of imagism, a kind of quick-fire verse I had not attempted before. I didn't use a camera, so I took poetry snapshots instead.

Recalling thirty years later the naive but open-hearted spirit of that collection, I knew that I must not let *Threading a Dream* become a Jungian tract or a dry anthropological study – and I definitely didn't want to end up sounding like that professor in the *Just William* story, whose hilariously dull lecture my elder daughter can still recite by heart: '*The earliest mention of Egypt in the Bible is under the name of Mizraim, which word most probably is a plural form testifying to the fact that Lower and Upper Egypt were regarded as distinct...*' Of experts on Egypt, there are plenty to be found; my expertise, such as it is, lies in directing the flow of words.

On one thing, however, I had made my mind up from the start. I would not begin my book as too many have before me, by quoting Herodotus's old chestnut, 'Egypt is the gift of the Nile'... although it is the Nile that threads this dream, and did somehow turn me into a poet.

MAP OF EGYPT

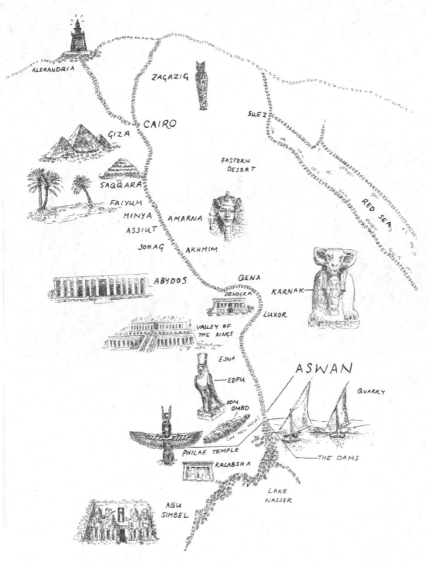

Threading a Dream

A Poet on the Nile

John Greening

Crossing

between haunches
baskets full of aubergine

the mothers

they rest their heads
their sickly bundles
on my shoes
or on my wife's thigh

the mothers
they surround us

hardly moving

a drum
hollow

muttering
bismillah!

hardly a breath

the ferry man
perhaps the father of a handful

though from the ditches in his face
the father
of a million
every year

fixes his narrow gaze on the bend
from which the breeze will come

we contemplate
a childless sky

and half a mile
of freedom

DATES

There was a good view of the desert from our neighbours' flat: the scree-like sweep of yellow down to the Nile – no fertile strip this far south – and the dark sockets of the Tombs of the Nobles. Near them, the Aga Khan's mausoleum, in which we had been told a fresh rose was placed every day, mysteriously. None of this had we visited yet. The sun was going down there on the west bank with its usual abruptness, but there were clouds, which was less usual. The High Dam and Lake Nasser behind it were meant to bring electricity to the people. Instead, they brought liver disease and rain. We were not really thinking about any of this. It had been a busy day of teaching and now we were rather looking forward to the Nile perch we were about to be offered. It had probably already been dished up, but custom held that food was allowed to cool before being presented to guests. We had yet to try the local fish, but fully expected it to be muddy in flavour. What we had seen of those perch, swimming among the rocks of the First Cataract, they looked more inclined to eat than be eaten.

Jane was the first to point out the distant flashes of light beyond the railway lines, over towards the eastern desert – a rockier, and much darker reddish landscape than across the river, rich in iron, a source of those vibrant brown colours in the tomb paintings. At first, we thought it must be something to do with shunting trains or wheels making sparks in the heat. But eventually we decided that it was lightning, although there was no thunder. No sooner had we agreed on this than there was a clattering and banging and shouting from somewhere outside. The long, broad mainstreet of Atlas was, like all Egyptian thoroughfares, extremely dusty, but the dust usually stayed where it was, stirred by the odd gust from the Nile, or kicked up by donkey carts, perhaps a *wallad* playing football. What we saw now was an enormous cloud of dust advancing down the street, bringing that same clattering and banging and shouting towards us.

We flew indoors as the building was engulfed. Dust was everywhere. The noise was terrific. Our hosts set to nailing up the shutters while the rest of us cowered in the flat. We had been planning to leave for the new university quarter out at 'Sahari City' that evening – one of many invitations we had not yet learnt how to refuse – but even the jeep that was ready to take us would not have coped with such conditions, so the driver was invited in and there we all sat. The storm raged – wind, rain, dust, great forks of lightning over to the east, though still no thunder. Next thing, the lights went out. Not an uncommon occurrence in Aswan, but when you're in an electric firestorm and on the fifth floor of a building constructed to resist nothing but sunshine, it's disconcerting. So we started singing: some Arabic songs and a few Coptic hymns from our hosts, and from us Good King Wenceslas.

It wasn't Christmas, but the so-called Suez holiday, one of countless special days in the Egyptian calendar when everything ground to a halt. No one would explain to us quite what Suez day celebrated, but I suspect it was something that Anthony Eden would rather not have heard. That we could be treated with such hospitality on a day which brought back memories of British aggression seems, in retrospect, remarkable. But at the time, other things were on our minds. It soon became apparent that this dust-storm had been a major event. Roads through to the Red Sea were closed. Refugees from the eastern desert started to appear on the outskirts of the Atlas estate. At least one local village was said to have been washed away and reports on the BBC a week later were mentioning as many as 20,000 people being made homeless between Aswan and the Red Sea. We learnt that sixty had been killed in our vicinity, mainly through electrocution – another of the gifts of the High Dam, a project whose dubious benefits we were to hear much more about as the months passed.

We had been in Upper Egypt for a few weeks when the storm hit; long enough for the first letters to have been exchanged with our families. Ten days out and ten days back was usually a good estimate for a response to anything sent by mail. And mail was the only way of communicating unless you were prepared to grapple with the post-office telephone booking system, which guaranteed nothing except frustration. So our parents would by now have heard of our epic journey on the 'Magarri', the train that follows the Nile over five hundred miles south from Cairo, along tracks laid down in the colonial era, and received our first impressions of the country we had been sent to as teachers by Voluntary Service Overseas. A two year posting. And there had been little choice in the matter. We were able to 'express a preference' and that preference, for our families' sakes, had been 'anywhere but the Middle East'. They sent us to Egypt. Admittedly, the country was in Peace mode,

4

since Anwar Sadat had just signed a historic accord with Israel. The streets were draped with banners depicting doves and olive branches. Sadat's and Jimmy Carter's smiling faces beamed at us from every lamp-post. Still, having mentally prepared ourselves for Papua New Guinea or other favourite VSO postings, it wasn't quite what we had expected.

News from our families was a vital matter. Less than six months earlier, on 29th April, our first wedding anniversary, we had been sitting holding glasses of champagne, about to drink a toast at my parents' home, when we received a phone-call to say that Jane's mother and grandfather had both had strokes. Her Grandpa Towers would die within the week. Her mother, Anne, made something of a recovery, but the question of our going abroad became a vexed one. 29th April had already established itself as a date to be negotiated with care since a close friend of Jane's family from their time in East Africa died on our wedding day. Now there seemed to be some sort of curse on it. And then, four days later, we heard that we were being sent to Upper Egypt.

It felt like the right decision as we settled in to our new lives and adapted to our celebrity status. We had been well prepared by VSO, so Jane knew to expect the pinching and poking in the street, the cries of 'Sophia Loren, Brigitte Bardot', the impossibility of ever being alone with a man, or even travelling with men in her university's minibus. And I had been briefed in the brutal ways of Egyptian school-teaching, the blackboards painted on mud-brick, the powdery chalk, the endemic cheating. We both had a smattering of colloquial Arabic – enough to shout 'have some respect' or 'I am a guest in your country'. And, more to the point, we were young, adaptable, and energetic. After the initial assault on our senses (both rancid and ravishing), after the realisation that we might as well take off our wristwatches and forget them, after coming to terms with the idea that privacy no longer meant a thing, after accepting that nothing – from matchsticks to fridges – would ever function as expected, we were beginning to enjoy ourselves. At first, there was a kind of homesickness. Among the books left behind by earlier volunteers was some poetry by Edward Thomas. This spell of service in Egypt was for me, I suppose, what joining the army had been for E.T., though I planned not to die in the effort to find my voice. Having written poetry since I was a student, I had still not found a way to sound convincingly myself, but in these exotic and extraordinary surroundings something was beginning to happen. I found myself reading Thomas and remembering the scents and textures of autumnal English countryside and began longing for footpaths 'winding like silver'. But even those we soon discovered.

As the aftermath of the storm died away, we made time one Friday (the Muslim day of prayer, our day off, when the air reverberated with *muezzin* and feedback) to go for a walk in the country, and the best place to do this was on the other side of the Nile – the west bank. As the local five piastre ferry (we shunned the tourist boat) took us across the half-mile stretch of Nile, we sat crammed up against the black-clad women with their palm-leaf baskets, their heaps of dried dates, their aromatic guavas and spices from the *souk*, and their even more aromatic goats and chickens. But for all the massing humanity aboard this little lateen-sailed boat, the feeling was of an unwonted calm, an Adlestrop moment which I attempted to capture in my poem 'Crossing', though Edward Thomas wouldn't have had a *tabla* player tapping meditatively in his carriage. The poem ends with the two of us contemplating 'a childless sky/and half a mile/of freedom'. Always the question we faced from strangers who got talking to us in their pidgin English or our creaky Arabic was why we had no children. *Lissa badri!* was our stock reply: there's still time! But time was not on Egyptian women's side. Their country boasts three calendars – the Islamic, the Coptic and the Western – but Egyptians go on ageing more quickly than most. Families had to have children while they could. The likelihood narrowed as the years passed, like that black strip beside the Nile. We knew a couple who were reduced to utter misery by their inability to conceive. Crocodile genitals were among the remedies considered. In time, when we were Westerners again, we would start a family: daughters, whom we have never taken out to 'The Black Land', as we ourselves have never returned. But at that particular time, there were children enough around us whenever we set off to walk beyond the tourist routes. *Baksheesh! Baksheesh!* came the cry.

The fertile strip beside the Nile at this point was no more than ten yards wide. There was only room for sporadic stands of date palms. The slope of sand that we had seen from our neighbours' flat now stretched above us for six or seven hundred feet, immaculate golden dunes. And on the other side (occasionally branching, buzzing with flies and wasps, over our heads) a dense undergrowth of thorns and numerous colourful, if inevitably dusty, plants and bushes. Squeezed into this narrow zone was an abundance of bird-life. Within a few minutes, apart from Aswan's familiar streetwise scavengers, the black kites, we had spotted a pied kingfisher, a bee-eater, with its flash of green-blue, and even what we suspected to be an osprey. There were egrets everywhere – still known as the ancient sacred ibis by locals – and hoopoes were as common as blackbirds at home. There were many moments during our time in Egypt that it seemed as if we had walked into a 3,000 year-old tomb painting, and this was one of them: that iconic scene in the British Museum collection of a bird-catcher astride his punt among the marshes, clutching three egrets and wielding a snake-headed stick. And indeed there were still bird-catchers, working their nets, much as there were fellahin collecting water from the river in their pivoting, counterbalanced *shadufs* as they had in pharaonic days. Talking to primary school-children about our visit when we were back in England, several of them seemed to think that we were actually ancient Egyptians. To be honest, it sometimes felt like it.

Certainly, time did not operate in any way that would have been recognisable to either Newton or Einstein. For one thing, the Islamic calendar begins its day at sunset, so every festival occurs earlier than you might expect, and converting from the Western to the Islamic system is a mysterious process (in short, divide the Islamic year by 33, subtract the result from the same year, then add 622, the date of Mohammed's flight from Mecca). Dates and times are of unparalleled significance in the Arab world, because they are so closely connected to the act of worship, but in social affairs it is altogether another matter. In English, there is no equivalent to *bukra* (pronounced bookra) although it is usually translated as simply 'tomorrow' and always qualified with what came to feel like a get-out clause: *ensha'allah* (God willing). There are many variations such as *bukra fil mish-mish* – 'tomorrow when the apricots bloom' – but essentially the Egyptian notion of tomorrow is any time after today. Therefore, inviting someone to visit tomorrow is like saying 'We must get together some time'. *Lissa* is another essential word – 'not yet': for buses, trains, supplies, the mail, our pay cheques and guests. In fact, to pin down a *Sa'idi* (an Upper Egyptian) to any particular date and time is all but impossible. In the early months, we had countless embarrassing misunderstandings over appointments and deadlines. Many a meal was prepared and abandoned because the guests did not appear.

And, as might be expected, the post also arrived erratically (*Lissa? Lissa!*), in non-linear sequence, particularly if it had once contained tasty or attractive gifts from home. But the intermeshing of our various pieces of news could become labyrinthine in a way that is hard to imagine now that much of the world has a smartphone. So it was that almost a month after the storm, we received a letter from my parents with a question from my mother, who has always had a psychic streak. She asked whether anything particularly momentous had happened on 25th October. She had suddenly had a strange instinct that something was wrong and she wondered... It was, of course, the night that we had been stranded in our neighbours' flat, the night a village was washed away.

A Date from Nubia

More than whisky warms
the heart on a balmless

February night,
Shukri, creaking to the gate

in a thin gallabiya
and a gone-home pair

of my old socks
warms it with his jokes

and his devilish winks
as he smiles '*ideeni* whisky!'

and we slap hands and laugh.
But he wouldn't touch the stuff,

he's a Nubian, the Koran
on his lap. In Ramadan

he won't swallow
his saliva, let alone

a scotch. When he prays,
it's five times down on his knees

at dawn, at noon,
in the afternoon, when the sun's

just gone, and in the evening.
If a stranger should ring

and interrupt him, he'll welcome
you with tea and then resume

from scratch, but only after
insisting you accept the offer

of a date – saying, except
fresh like gold dropped

from the palm you could chew
to the breathing of the buffalo

water wheels, he has no taste
for them himself; but a guest

like you, who's off
to Abu Simbel or to photograph

the High Dam, must eat
one dried date

as a commemorative act:
the last time dates were picked

in Nubia, Shukri had
teeth, and Nasser wasn't dead.

HOMES

We did not realise it at the time, but the destruction of those villages in the desert was just another of the junctures when our life in Egypt would force us to confront the very notion of home. So long as we were actually travelling, disorientation and discomfort had been part of the experience. The *Pension Roma* in Cairo, where there were plenty of bed-bugs and mosquitoes but no running water, had almost been fun. On the seventeen-hour train journey south – long before we had actually met any bedouin – we imagined ourselves as Yeats's 'Arab tribesman and his tent', heading down to the Tropic of Cancer, the bobbing *shadufs* and donkey-carts of sugar cane glimpsed from the window like an exotic dream. 'Welcome at Aswan' the signs had read as we spilled out of the train into the glare from one of the hottest places on earth, where Africa at last began to assert itself, the southernmost extent of the Roman empire.

At least we were volunteers. The poet Juvenal is said to have been banished to Aswan in the second century AD as a punishment for his scurrilous satirical attacks on the regime. He was appointed prefect of the garrison at Syene, the settlement which would become Aswan, and obliged to defend the remotest border of an empire which he had mocked. Was he sent to Egypt because he had expressed particular contempt for Egyptians in his poetry or was that contempt bred while he was stuck in Upper Egypt? He is a good shade to have had at my elbow in those years, a reminder that lines of verse can sometimes get under the skins of politicians, that words have unpredictable powers, that there can be more to poetry than mists and mellow fruitfulness. Had I known it when we were out there, I would also surely have sympathised with the opening to his very first Satire: 'Why is it I always have to hear other people reciting and can't be up there reading myself?'

Our new home proved to be away from the centre of town in a fairly modern estate originally built for the families of Russian engineers working on the High Dam. Atlas had a forbidding eastern-bloc feel to it. Still, the flat itself was positively luxurious by local standards and appeared to be well equipped, though initially with a kitchen full of beds and without fridge or fan. Nor was there any hot water – cold showers were the norm and soap was unavailable because of a national shortage. What we had not learnt on that late September day as Shukri unlocked the door for us was that even in the land of the pyramids any abundance is temporary, and permanence is an illusion. In fact, the nature of Egyptian life is better reflected by the metaphor of the inundation: obliteration, transformation, improvisation... And the one essential word for survival is *maleesh* – never mind, that's the way it is, or (in the language of a later century), 'whatever...' It's a good thing that we did not know as we stood there with Shukri that a few months later, on Christmas Day, just as we were feeling thoroughly settled, and relishing our sense of belonging, there would be a tap on our door and a functionary would announce that we were moving house *bukra*. Like the apricots, that particular *bukra* never came.

Egyptian mod cons often look like the real thing but really aren't. So, just as we were dropping into bed after our first day of battling Soviet-style bureaucracy, trying to ignore the howling of the dogs outside our window (they roamed the estate in packs at night) I noticed that the cistern in the bathroom was making a lot of noise. After much negotiation with the ballcock, it was back to bed, switch out the light. But the light stayed on, flickering and fizzing. Assuming there was a problem with the switch, we moved to the second of the three bedrooms. Same problem. *This isn't your home*, it fizzed, *this isn't your home*. The light, it appeared (gift of the High Dam that suppressed the inundation) could never be turned off. At least bedroom number three had a species of darkness, although it also had a species of cricket in the skirting boards, and once the dogs outside had settled, we were at last on the verge of falling into a hot uncomfortable sleep. It was then that the toilet started flushing by itself.

So had begun our attempt to make a new home beside the First Cataract of the Nile, where granite pushes through the sandstone before the river's final advance towards the Delta. We were incredibly lucky to have been sent to this favourite holiday location. We knew volunteers in the Delta and in various less salubrious parts of Egypt and there was a good deal of discontent. Aswan was deep into Africa and could be very hot, but crucially it did not have the humidity of Lower Egypt and around Christmas offered the healthiest climate in North Africa. Nor were there the social problems of cities further downriver, the tensions between Copt and Muslim, the social disorder. There were no conurbations, no sprawling slums. When food riots happened, it would be in Assiut or Sohag, not Aswan. Aswanis liked their town and we quickly felt at home,

14

chiefly through the many invitations we had to the homes of others. The visit to our neighbours, where we experienced the storm, was just one of dozens of calls we found ourselves making on the enthusiastic middle classes – very often Copts, who wanted to stake their claim as fellow Christians (even if we weren't exactly) as much as their status as the true descendants of the pharaohs. There was a kind of chain reaction that would take place, often following encounters in the street or help with negotiation over prices in the *souk*, which would lead to a friendly chat, a glass of *karkodeh* (hibiscus flower), or *tamarahindi*, or pomegranate juice and an invitation to call. But the most memorable were the homes of the poorer people, particularly our *maquaggi*, Asmi.

A *maquaggi* is someone who does laundry (like a *dhobi* in India) and to watch this gentle, softly-spoken old man, dressed in the customary gallabiya, hard at work ironing our clothes in his mud-brick 'shop' was quite an experience. No steam-iron for him, but a set of solid implements which he heated on a stove. He would then take a mouthful of water and with unfailing accuracy and surprising range, spray what he was ironing from his pursed lips. Never had my scruffy old shirts been given such tender loving care. Asmi, who had been ironing for volunteers for many years was one of Egypt's few Roman Catholics but there was none of the aggressive anti-Muslim talk from him, only humble attention to our attempts at speaking Arabic. Visiting his house in those early weeks is still clear in my memory. At the time it suggested what 'blessed are the poor' might actually mean, even if Asmi himself was clearly ambitious to improve himself. We sat in his living room drinking hot sweet tea, the untwinkling stars – why would he have needed a roof? – shining down on us, the gekkos scampering across his walls, clucking and occasionally jumping on to us. There was a prominently displayed single bare light-bulb as he had just had electricity 'installed'. There were sweetmeats. A crucifix. His wife and daughters appeared from the shadows, and smiled and giggled at Jane. It was only because of her presence that they were allowed out – our fellow volunteers, Alan and Stuart, were astonished at the females beginning to appear now that there was a married woman in town. Asmi remained a good friend even after the day he visited us and was invited to make himself comfortable next to a bundle of fresh laundry from a rival *maquaggi* (who was nearer and cheaper). The moustache did not even quiver. He had the dignity not to notice the fact that we had temporarily abandoned him.

15

If the Copts prided themselves on their authenticity, the oldest inhabitants of Aswan were the Nubians, with their distinctly African features and jet-black skin. Nubia proper begins south of Aswan and has always been remote, more so since Kitchener's railway to Khartoum veered off into the desert rather than following the Nubian bend of the Nile. Old rails (made in Birmingham) would turn up as beams among the split palm-wood in the houses now beneath Lake Nasser at the same time as other elements of their homes dated back to Roman times, notably their ingenious wooden latches. Since there is barely any naturally fertile land so far upriver, the *Nubee* have always had to make do with what they could find, and they found that the date palm could provide some forty different products. But many sought work elsewhere, sending money back to the families they were supporting. All the *bowabs* or 'porters' at our block of flats had come from Old Nubia, displaced by the rising waters behind the High Dam. This was a scandalous business that we only gradually learnt about, but I would make it the subject of my stage play, High Dam, written while we were in Aswan. It is set in the 1960s, and begins like this:

SHERIF, *the director of operations at the High Dam,* AHMED *an enumerator, and* HANNAH, *a Californian journalist, are seen standing on the 'dam'. This is a tall screen the width of the stage with a walkway and a narrow ladder leading down to stage left. Bright lights shine above the three characters, who have their backs to the audience. They are looking down (upstage) behind the dam to where the construction work is going on, suggested by shadows on the screen and noise of excavation. There are wind sound effects, too. A jeep is at the foot of the screen, far left. On the opposite side, right, squats an* OLD NUBIAN MAN. *He is preparing tea on a little kerosene burner.*

SHERIF: (*back to the audience, bellowing against noise*) When it is completed, this wall where we stand will reach a height of more than a hundred metres. It will be a thousand metres in width and three kilometres from the east bank to the west bank! It will be known as the *Saad-el-Aali* – the High Dam! (*he pauses for effect.* AHMED *turns round to face the audience and yawns.*) It will be seventeen times greater than the Great Pyramid.

16

(AHMED *starts to climb bulkily and clumsily down the ladder.* HANNAH *turns round and watches, more amused by this sight than* SHERIF's *talk.*)

HANNAH: Well. (*She follows* AHMED *down*)

SHERIF: (*Not turning round*) The reservoir lake where the River Nile meets this concrete mountain will be four hundred kilometres long and an average of fifteen kilometres wide. It will contain four thousand million cubic feet of water!

(*Noise of machinery and wind fades out as* OLD NUBIAN MAN *carries a tray of tea over to the ladder and starts to climb. Silence.*)

AHMED: (*Innocently*) And the Nubian man, Ustaz Sherif? Tell us...

(*Silence as* SHERIF *turns to face audience from the dam. He looks momentarily shifty, then sighs, takes his tea. The* OLD NUBIAN MAN *squats on the walkway.*)

SHERIF: You know... these people, they are very poor. They have nothing. Their mind is little. They were slaves...

AHMED: (*Quietly*) Come, Miss Hannah.

(*She does not move immediately, but* AHMED *goes to the jeep and sits in it.*)

SHERIF: They will be moved to better places on new land that will be irrigated. Modern houses, modern hospitals, employment, electricity...

AHMED: Come, Miss Hannah.

HANNAH: (*Calls up*) Thank you, Mr...

SHERIF: Ten thousand million kilowatt hours every year from twelve turbines...

AHMED: (*to* HANNAH) Sherif. It mean 'honest'.

HANNAH: Mr Sherif.

AHMED: (*letting her into the jeep but not getting out to do it*) Everything about this dam big. Now it is the biggest *hole* you ever see!

(*They laugh and are about to drive off, when there is an explosion. Blackout. Then, spot on the jeep and the startled pair. Offstage, sounds of a siren and vague silhouettes of bodies being removed. Into the spot a sheaf of papers is tossed from the walkway.*)

SHERIF: (*Calls from above*) Names! (*And another sheaf*) Letters!

(AHMED *takes these, gets into jeep again, shaking head and begins to drive. Nubian music begins: a mournful piping, becoming more cheerful and accompanied by moving images from Nubia on the screen of the 'dam' as* AHMED *talks to his passenger:*)

AHMED: I tell you the truth about Nubian man, Miss Hannah. They are in Egypt since the beginning. Before many time there are even Pharaoh from Nubia. You see this land – they are still live in this place. Since the beginning.

HANNAH: But there's nothing here, Ahmed.

AHMED: Look, Miss Hannah, look all round.

HANNAH: Desert. *Desert.* Well, I guess the Nile somewhere over there, and – and dates – but –

AHMED: Without this date, there is no Nubia. They use this for all thing. Food, drinking, wood for their house, cloth for

their dressing, rope for their sakkiya... Listen. (*a faint creaking*)
Ah, the sakkiya. Their buffalo drive this water wheel. You shall
hear this everywhere. It never end, this... (*It fades*) It is the
sound that history make because she is trapped. It is a sound so
old like Nubia herself. (*No sound, the images from Nubia have
gone. Only water lapping insidiously in the background.*) When
the new lake come, the sound will stop. History begin to free
herself. All this will go. All you will see is water.   *Blackout.*

The real drama had been enacted decades before we were there, when
some three thousand of the original forty-two thousand residents of the
Wadi Halfa area refused to leave their homes. They set up a shanty town
in the desert near the shores of the lake where old Wadi Halfa had been,
with its celebrated stands of date palms and its historical sites such as
the Coptic church and Kitchener's house. Eventually the governments
of Sudan and Egypt agreed to let them stay and so New Wadi Halfa was
born and the railway was even extended to their settlement.

 The Nubian porters Yussef, Adli and toothless Shukri himself
would bring us our half kilo of buffalo milk to be boiled, alert us when
the egg man was coming with his minuscule eggs (almost entirely yolk)
and fetch us white *fino* bread or the cheaper *balladi* if we couldn't
face the throng. We were always uncomfortable with this servant/
master situation, but sometimes sheer necessity forced us to revert to
such practices. Before we came to Egypt, we had been teased by Jane's
father and a friend of his from East Africa that we were becoming neo-
colonials. Reading Lord Edward Cecil's 1921 memoir, *The Leisure of an
Egyptian Official* – a favourite with volunteers – we would come across
disconcertingly familiar anecdotes, even as we gasped at the racism in the
humour. It wasn't so much the descriptions of Cecil's servant that struck
a chord ('after years of careful practice, he has discovered how to drop a
woollen garment on a thick carpet and make it sound like a plank falling
on a pavement.') as the accounts of everyday street life:

 The early tram runs off the line five days in seven. I watch it as
 it approaches, and, sure enough, it goes off the line and pulls
 up. The driver carefully gets on the brake, and spreading his
 hands before him in the national gesture of expostulation and
 complaint, calls Heaven to witness that he is an unlucky man,

and that the company treats him like a dog. The conductor, who has dismounted, joins in, and they continue to bewail their lot until the conductor hints that the driver was in fault. The driver replies hotly that he was not, adding that the conductor's relations are not respectable. The passengers, who have also dismounted, form a circle round the two, and after listening to a short biographical sketch of the driver by the conductor, take sides, and the row becomes general. As the voices become shriller and shriller in the fury of the quarrel, which has all the appearance of being about to lead to bloodshed, and which, in reality, would never lead to the lightest blow, a sleepy policeman approaches the group. Every one appeals to him, and he, with great impartiality, abuses every one. He, however, has the sense to suggest that the tram ought to go on. The driver and the conductor, still raging, admit this, and with the assistance of the crowd shove the car back on to the lines in that hopelessly unmethodical and eminently successful manner pursued by Egyptians when dealing with heavy weights. The driver and conductor take their places, the passengers scramble back to their seats, and the car jolts away into the distance.

Cecil also gives a vivid portrait of his boss, Lord Kitchener. Every day in Aswan we looked across to what was known as Kitchener's Island, where the man with the moustache and the pointing finger had planned his assault on the Sudan. It was difficult, then, to entirely forget the imperial legacy and it's also true that one of the attractions of this tour was to recapture some of the magic that Jane associated with her childhood in Tanganyika and Zanzibar. Her father had been a District Officer and then private secretary to the Sultan. My own father, by contrast, worked in the Home Office as a civil servant. Our two backgrounds were very different, although while we were away our families did get together to exchange letters, listen to cassettes we had made and have slide-shows.

Naturally, Jane was very concerned about her mother while we were away. Her collapse was the culmination of years of drinking and is the darker side to the story of colonial decline. The Woodland family had had to abandon their world and settle in suburban London. No longer the cocktail parties and 'White Mischief' values. It is no wonder that this star-struck Cockney girl could not cope when the glamour and the celebrity and the power vanished from her life. All that was left was the drink. Jane never drank, which made the alcohol-free life in Aswan easy for her to adapt to, but there was so much in the everyday sights and sounds and smells of our new home that reminded her of her childhood. Africa had worked its way into the *souks* here, with the heaped multi-coloured spices (saffron, paprika, cayenne) and umpteen varieties of date and obscure fruit such as *doum*, vegetables like 'lady's fingers', aubergine, sweet potato, rocket and *mulukhia*, the reeking, half-rotted guava and mango, the gigantic, allegedly sewage-fed watermelons, tiny bunches of green bananas, green lemons and green navel oranges (*bi-surra*); it hung in the bougainvillea, jasmine, hibiscus flowers, the 'bomb trees' (did we ever learn their proper name?) and ever-present date palms.

As my poem 'A Date from Nubia' suggests, those dates were the reserve of Nubian culture, and the New Nubia settlement represented a complete deracination of the people from their multi-purpose trees. But one of the most distinctive elements of Nubian life was, I believe, preserved in the resettlement programme: the design of their houses. The whitewashed tunnel vaulting creates a natural air conditioning. Those who had made the pilgrimage to Mecca (and not only Nubians) would paint murals of the event on the outsides of these brilliant white homes, so very often on the edge of the desert, among the goats and the detritus, one's eye would be drawn to the brightly coloured image of a jumbo jet. Occasionally, we would go out to the Nubian settlement on the outskirts of Aswan – an old-established one rather than the neatly regimented New Nubia complex which was downstream, near Kom Ombo – and we were always struck by the unthreatening nature of this very poor quarter. The Nubians are a meditative people, much more formal and restrained. Our friend Hassan had a single copy of Dr Johnson's *Lives of the Poets* (he lacked volume two) in his tunnel-vaulted dwelling. He also had more cockroaches than I have ever been close to when the lid was lifted off his earth latrine for my benefit. His house was fairly typical, but didn't have the colourful painting, brilliant flat basketwork wall-hangings and embedded pieces of china plates we would see in more rural Nubian homes and which were the style before the High Dam. I wonder now whether Hassan knew Johnson's version of the tenth Satire by that sometime Aswani poet, Juvenal:

Let Observation with extensive View
Survey Mankind from China to Peru;
Remark each anxious Toil, each eager Strife,
And watch the busy Scenes of crowded Life;
Then say how Hope and Fear, Desire and Hate,
O'erspread with Snares the clouded Maze of Fate,
Where wav'ring Man, betray'd by vent'rous Pride,
To tread the dreary Paths without a Guide;
As treacherous Phantoms in the Mist delude,
Shuns fancied Ills, or chases airy Good.

In my role as visiting teacher, I would have to take myself off to Nubian schools every now and then ('without a Guide'). The school in West Aswan was the most memorable, not least for the Nile crossing, which is by far the pleasantest commute I have ever made. Several of the teachers whose classes I sat in on also made this journey every morning from the tourist 'corniche', where the inappropriately clad Westerners wandered. I never forgot that in stepping on to that ferry to the west bank I was visiting the ancient home of the dead, who were also known as the Westerners. It was this double meaning that gave me the title of my first book. Even before we came to Aswan I had been preoccupied with last things, particularly keen on elegy, on those artists who drew inspiration from consciousness of their extinction: the symphonist Bruckner, for example, or the Schubert of *Winterreise*, certain Symbolist painters, or poets like Donne and Yeats (who claimed that there were only two subjects fit for poetry: sex and the dead). But here in Upper Egypt, young though we were, death was woven into our daily existence. It was in the faces shuttling from one side of the Nile to the other. It was in the tombs on the horizon. It was in the very dust we all breathed. Yet it felt most insidiously present when our own 'Western' values imposed themselves on the time-honoured Egyptian way. When a flashy tour boat swept through. Or someone's TV played *Dynasty*. Crossing the Nile was always a time to reflect: perhaps on such matters; perhaps simply on the next refreshment stop; perhaps on the possibility of spotting a Nile Monitor, those large predatory lizards that substitute for hippo and croc; perhaps on where precisely that well was located that Eratosthenes came from Alexandria to find – the one where the sun's rays entered vertically at the solstice – so he could measure the earth's circumference. I could have asked one of the Maths teachers on the ferry with me. (Eratosthenes's estimate was only 242km out.)

At 7 a.m., heat was not yet a problem and it was an unmathematical pleasure to sit following the shore around the bend away from Aswan. I could see the farmers at work, cattle and buffalo grazing, tethered donkeys, the odd camel. I could see groups of boys clutching satchels, winding their way towards the school on the backs of donkeys and other clusters of darker-skinned boys washing in the river. There would be a black-clad woman or two scrubbing out a pan in the Nile or doing the laundry and always something unexpected – some creature or crop I'd not noticed before. A new mother following Nubian custom by presenting her baby to the sun, or an old man placing a pot of water on a grave for the birds (that is to say, for the souls). Soon we were at the muddy bank that was the disembarkation point for West Aswan School. From here there was a good long hike to the edge of the fertile strip. Dry mud paths inbetween fields of *ful* beans and cotton, then into the date groves. A Nubian man picks up a few dates left over from the recent harvest, offers me one. *Etfaddal!* (And of course, the astonished *Betekállem Arabi? You speak Arabic?*) I take it. *Kwai'yes!* Dry, but delicious, like toffee. You could see all the dates spread out to mellow in the sun. Nubian dates were then as now Aswan's main crop and they were the best in Egypt. People say the same of the peanuts. But there were various other things grown, too, so there was extensive irrigation and I would often pass a creaking *sakkiya* that supplied the fields with Nile water. The school itself was a tumbledown collection of buildings grouped around a small courtyard that served as a quad. The pupils would be already assembled there, standing to attention, now at ease, attention again. They stamped their feet smartly, shouted the national slogan three times, then marched away to the beating of a drum. Every one of them was a Nubian, but the national anthem they sang was, of course, Egyptian.

If the Nubians came to represent a displaced people whose cause has been wholly overlooked, whose homeland is gone forever beneath the onrush of development, then the Bisharin stood for all those who never had (or perhaps wanted) a home. These were our nearest nomads. The Bisharin did in fact have somewhere they could touch base on the edge of Aswan near Asmi's shop and our friend Ibrahim once took us to visit them. That was our first experience of coffee à la Bisharin, a ceremony lasting almost an hour, which involved taking fresh coffee beans, roasting them in front of us over glowing charcoal on a specially laid out rug, then grinding them in a hand mortar. Add hot water and root ginger and the result is a cup – or three or five or seven – of extremely strong black coffee. It's unlucky to have an even number of cups and when you've had enough you have to show it by turning your cup upside down on the tray. This was our first experience of this ceremony, and curiously we witnessed it again shortly afterwards in even more atmospheric circumstances.

We had been on a trip out into the desert with some development workers who were trying to encourage cultivation of some of the bleak new shores around Lake Nasser. We were tens of miles from any settlement, at the far end of the newly drowned Wadi Allaki. Our Russian botanist friend, Ira, wanted to collect plants – this was a happy hunting ground for her – and the man from CARE just wanted to see if anything was happening here. But he hoped he might be able to take us to the legendary tribal leader, Gar el Nabi. The valley's broad greenish terrain (it felt very African) was until recently desert, but it was where the nomads traditionally met to exchange camels and whatever else they had brought up from the Sudan. In pharaonic times, it had been the main route to the gold mines in Kush, but now it was right on the fringes of everything, yet very fertile and ripe for development. Steve, the CARE representative, knew that the nomadic people of this area were likely to be missing out on the opportunities available, and projects such as extending the railway through here would be unlikely to benefit them.

There were about seventy Bisharin in the valley now, Steve told us as our jeep sped across the floodplain. And even as he spoke we saw an old man run towards us, waving, having emerged apparently out of nowhere. He wore a sand-coloured (once white) gallabiya with a white turban. He had bright friendly eyes and a relaxed voice. This was Gar el Nabi. He didn't seem like a man of the desert at all; only in one or two mannerisms did it appear that he differed from any other *Sa'idi*. He would barely shake hands with Jane, for example, and looked away as he did so. And then there was the coffee ceremony again, this time beneath palm-frond-covered metal poles literally in the middle of the desert. Dung beetles crawled hither and thither as we sat. Herons circled and headed off north. We scanned the horizon for gazelles and ostriches. Apart from this resting place, there were only a few tents – curious box-shaped arrangements made from skins – stretching along the valley. Here the women could be seen in their sandy dresses, kept at a safe distance from travellers. Jane went and spoke to them and was interested to hear about their various customs. Her diary describes their unbleached cotton garments, their plaited hair, gold nose-rings and the liberal use of kohl (even on babies). They gave her sweet tea and took her to see the harem. There was a not unpleasant smell about the women, she said, which couldn't be put down to the fat they rub in their hair. She decided it must be the coal tar which they distil themselves and remarked that my father, a longtime enthusiast for Wrights Coal Tar Soap, would approve. Had I caught a breath of that in the desert, I suspect that it would have whisked me a very long way home.

The Black Land

in variegated heaps
in a field
in the sun

dates...

and other dried fruit
thresh dust
blacken
obeying a plough
urging primordial buffalo
to work the cogged wheel another season

all
unalterable

except
forty million
are on the fly-strip

buzz
jostle

trachoma in empty eyes
bilharzia in full blood

the old red bus
bursting heat
and huge *sa'idi* grins
will continue to shudder
through the shabby hens
and urchins

some black old women
get down

their home
their whole village
barely emerging
from sandstone

invisible
at more than donkey-speed

a tunnel vault
a turreted wall
whitewash
with poster colours
of a Boeing
lumbering off to Mecca

The Great, the Step, and Other Pyramids

If the High Dam rather than the Great Pyramid has dominated our horizon, it's because we were living nearly a thousand kilometres upriver from Giza and a good way from any pyramid at all. We did visit the national honeypot several times, but we prided ourselves on remaining aloof. Just as we mocked those who brazenly strolled hand in hand along the corniche of our adopted town, venturing no further than the facade of souvenir shops, the women bare-armed, the men in skimpy shorts, so there was something in the spirit of volunteering that made us sniff at the obvious icon. I do have a memory of being whisked out to Giza during our first days in Cairo, feeling overcome by heat and culture shock, incapable of reacting adequately to my first Ancient Wonder and generally being unmoved by the location. Even in 1979, you had to make sure you only looked in one direction if you wanted to preserve any illusion of lone and level sands. Modern development – chiefly the hotel industry – has pushed right up to the very edge of the sacred site. We may complain about the way Stonehenge loses its remote, prehistoric atmosphere because of the roads on either side; the Pyramids of Giza are far worse, no longer encountered in the desert, but in the suburbs.

Two things are worth noting. Firstly, that the pyramid is a very useful metaphor for much of the way Egyptian society operated when we were there: every organisation had its pharaoh and its slaves. I suspect that, long after the assassination of Sadat and despite the revolution, there is still a desire to look up to a flashy golden capstone. Meanwhile, 40% of the country's wealth is controlled by 5% of the population and the agricultural worker who leaves the land for a factory will not earn in a lifetime what each of Egypt's richest 100,000 spend on a single car. Secondly, there are pyramids as well as Pyramids – i.e. they exist at many other sites than Giza. At the last count there were 138 of them and, following some revelatory satellite surveys, that number is set to increase dramatically. Each has its own peculiarities: step pyramid, bent pyramid, shining pyramid, collapsed pyramid... Even obelisks were once considered pyramids, as in Shakespeare's Sonnet 123 ('No! Time, thou shalt not boast that I do change, / Thy pyramids built up with newer might / To me are nothing novel, nothing strange, / They are but dressings of a former sight') where the reference is in fact to a set of obelisks dug up on the orders of the Pope and erected in Rome in the 1580s.

The decision any visitor to Giza must make (apart from how decisively they should reject offers of a camel ride) is whether to go inside the Great Pyramid of Cheops, or Khufu as he is generally known these days. On both occasions that we visited, Jane and I decided we wouldn't and sometimes I have regretted this. The earliest descriptions of the interior conjure the most bizarre and fanciful possibilities. The Arab writer Masoudi, for example related in the tenth century AD:

> The chamber walls were composed of small square stones of beautiful colours; and a person, having put one of these stones in his mouth, was suddenly seized with a pain in his ears, which continued until he had replaced it. They also discovered in a large hall a quantity of gold coins piled in columns, each coin the weight of a thousand dinars. They tried to take the money but were unable to move it. In another place they found the image of a sheikh, made of green stone, sitting upon a sofa and wrapped in a garment. Before him were statues of little boys, whom he was occupied in instructing....

After which close encounter with a petrified teacher, they meet a cock made of precious stones, whose eyes illuminate the chamber as it flaps its wings and crows. Flinders Petrie, the greatest Egyptologist of modern times, is a safer guide, writing exactly one hundred years before our own first visit, and with an excavator's eye for the precise detail even at the age of twenty-six:

> After getting up and breakfast, I went off with Ali to the Pyramid. There had been a good deal of rain in the night, and it lay on rocky parts and in pools in the plain, it had also run in and filled the footholes cut in the descending passage... went into the Queen's Chamber and then up the Grand Gallery to the King's Chamber. Crawled into all the length of [Colonel Richard] Vyse's cut by the air channel, and saw that the bottom end of it is clear, but there was no draught in it. Then in the King's Chamber I measured the joints of the bottom course of the north wall...and then took sundry measures in the ante-

chamber... I found the smell of bats very unpleasant but got used to it. The heat was too much for working in, and I took off hat and coat at first...

He ends up working through the night without any clothes, desperate to salvage all the archaeology he can. He wrote later that 'the science of observation, of registration, of recording was as yet unthought of' and his work 'was like a house on fire, so rapid was the destruction going on'.

Destruction is the subtext to all discussions of Egyptian antiquities, and it's easy to forget how much at Giza had already been looted even by the time of Masoudi. Before local people saw it as an easy house-building resource rather than a sacred tomb, the Great Pyramid would have been clad in dazzling white limestone. The stones we see now were only the inner lining. Climbing that wall of stones might have been an attractive option when we were there and I can't remember whether it was forbidden or not. It would have been an uncomfortable choice between claustrophobia and vertigo. What a visitor really wants to do is stand for a very long time without being troubled by vendors and beggars and tour guides, and try and take in that *These Are the Pyramids*. Is it, in fact, better not to actually see them, but to let them exist unpolluted in the imagination? Wordsworth felt something similar when he saw the 'soulless image' of Mont Blanc and felt it had (as he put it in *The Prelude*) 'usurp'd upon a living thought/That never more could be'. Close up they seemed less real, I remember thinking, than they did on widescreen films, in glossy coffee-table books, on posters and cigarette ads. Paradoxically, the further we got from them, the more palpable they seemed. Glimpsed between buildings in Giza, they were manageably vast. Seen from below, in the desert, the brain couldn't process them.

There are so many snatches of pyramidia in my head – anecdotes, legends mingling with startlingly few facts – that it's impossible to know which are important. Colonel Vyse's dynamite assault in 1837. Von Däniken's alien visitors. Circus strongman Belzoni stuck in a passageway. Alignments to the constellation Orion. Aleister Crowley's honeymoon night in the King's Chamber. There was one TV programme in which a robot camera was sent up formerly unexplored passageways, and another which used computer graphics to dramatise building methods. There have been the numerous theories about how the physical labour was managed (sledges, ramps, rollers, winches, square-levels, A-frames) including reconstructions and re-enactments. I have read many a John Romer and all the Leonard Cotterells, whose popular archaeological guides became favourites of ours, but I also tackled the classic blue Pelican paperback by Keeper of Egyptian Antiquities at the British Museum, I.E.S. Edwards, *The Pyramids of Egypt*. Nothing beside remains. Humiliatingly, I retain much more about the New Age fads such as how to make a cardboard pyramid to sharpen razor blades, keep milk fresh (or mummify a dead cat). And I know, because I later wrote a long poem about it, how Dorothy Eady of Blackheath, who called herself Omm Sety, came to Giza in the 1930s, convinced that she had been the consort of Sety I in a former life, and awoke one night to find that she had been lured out by her ghostly lover to climb the Great Pyramid.

A glance at any of the hundreds of Pyramid books will give the facts that never fail to astound: the 2.3 million blocks of stone, each weighing two and a half tons, used by Khufu's builders; or Napoleon's calculation that the three Giza Pyramids, if dismantled, could be reconstructed as a foot-thick wall, ten feet high, around the the entire perimeter of France (reduced to a row of twelve inch cubes it would go two-thirds of the way round the earth). Then there is the accuracy of the workmanship, first established by Flinders Petrie. Khufu's structure incorporates four perfect right-angles and the angle of each slope is precisely 51° 50' 40", all four slopes identical to within two inches of each other.

It helps also to think of the importance of the site chosen: a plateau of limestone, the Mokattam Formation, which provided the raw material for that casing, long stripped away. The Khufu Quarry, as it is called, is a few hundred yards from the Pyramids, but was barely known about until the early twentieth century. Yet here most of those two-and-a-half ton stones were hacked out (by today's best computation, assuming it took twenty-three years to construct, a labour force of some twelve hundred men) then dragged uphill. It's generally agreed that there were wooden tracks, lubricated with water, to assist the process, which would have needed another two-and-a-half thousand men. Then a further seven hundred did the actual building.

Although such analyses do help one appreciate the Pyramids, so did little unexpected things such as seeing Egyptian workmen toiling on a building site for a new hotel. For lack of a JCB they would use a shovel with a long date-palm rope attached, and a line of labourers would all haul together as the man holding the shovel swung it. I can imagine a similar technique being used at Giza. Khufu's Wonder of the World became most real for me, I think, when I was standing not in the limestone quarry at Giza, but at the other end of Egypt in Aswan's old granite quarry (see my poem, 'The Crack', p. 102). It is a unique and little visited place, abandoned millennia ago but remaining just as it must have been – a half-finished obelisk not yet removed from the rock, chippings and offcuts lying about, slots and notches seemingly freshly cut. As I stood among all the prehistoric detritus, I could at last begin to conceive how four and a half thousand years ago this beautiful pink and grey material was excavated and transported down the Nile and hauled to Giza to line the 'burial' chamber for Khufu. Nine huge horizontal slabs of granite from Aswan make up the ceiling and more four rows of similar slabs hold off the entire mass of the Great Pyramid from crushing whoever or whatever was in the chamber. Lying on the shelf beside me as I type, I have a roughly triangular, sandwich-sized chunk of this pink granite picked from that same quarry. It glitters even in the sunless light of an English summer's day. You can see the marks made where the wooden wedges were inserted and dampened in order to split the rock. If I believed in psychometry (and I once met a man in Cornwall who practised it) I might almost expect to see a vision of labouring hordes as I hold it, running my fingers over the craggy surface, taking the rough with the smooth.

It was the much earlier step pyramid at Saqqara that made the most enduring impression and even that was because of what lay next to it: the labyrinth of the Serapeum. The occasion of our visit was a relaxing one, too, in the company of Dave and Pamela, who were friends associated with the British Council and based in Ain Shams, a suburb of Cairo. One Friday late in May they drove us out of the city (being in a car that wasn't a taxi was in itself a pleasure) and into the palm groves, pyramid-spotting all the way – there was Giza, at a safe and manageable and believable distance – then on towards the Third Dynasty, to this oldest stone building of any size in the world, Djoser's Step Pyramid. Effectively it's an early attempt, by the architect and high-priest Imhotep, at the technique of pyramid building in which the design is more like the kind of tower a child might make from squares of ever-decreasing size, starting with what is known as a mastaba, which means 'bench' in Arabic: a low memorial platform. The idea seems to have been a staircase into the sky, but this may be a case of making necessity the mother of excuses. Once architects worked out (in the Fourth Dynasty) how to disguise the steps and make the sides smooth, the pyramid shape we recognise today emerged. There are several other pyramids in the vicinity in varying states of decay. What stays most vividly in my imagination (apart from the Serapeum) is not the 'early reliefs and paintings' that I mention in a letter, 'walls packed with action and, once upon a time, colour', nor the 'Pyramid Texts inside the Pyramid of Unas (collapsed) which are the earliest known version of *The Book of the Dead*', but sitting nervously under a makeshift awning as we waited for tea or cola, while pye dogs from the desert loped in and out unchallenged like the advance guard of Anubis.

But if we are thinking about which particular pyramid had most immediate effect on our lives in Egypt, it must be the Pyramid of Bureaucracy. Most of our time was spent among the toiling slaves who build the never-to-be completed edifice – the poor, illiterate, sickly, underpaid fellahin and their women who carried everything for them on their heads, from sewing machines to great canisters of *butagas*. We had experience of the miserable labyrinthine passageways of its middle reaches, offices where clerks were trapped for a lifetime, desk upon desk of them; tier upon tier of red-taped authority; even in the schools and universities this was the case. And whenever we needed permission to do anything or go anywhere, then we were called to the government's Kafkaesque administrative headquarters in Cairo, known as the *Mugamma*. As for the sunlit upper slopes of the Pyramid of Bureaucracy, it was fascinating to see how the man near the top, such as our local Governor, who left us sitting in his office and ignored us for two hours when we first arrived, would suddenly become the gleaming golden welcomer when we brought influential people from the British Council. Doubtless this would happen anywhere in the world, but in Egypt the gulf between high and low, rich and poor, seemed as extreme as the gulf between fertile strip and desert – and 94% of the land is desert.

Pyramids

at four each morning
the mosque loudspeaker
calls Egyptians –

a howling desert dog
disturbing
the tour groups
from their sun-baked
hotel bedroom slumber

but the call
and the howl
that have reverberated
through to the earth's far side
since morning

the megaphones of
Menkau-Rē
Khaef-Rē
Khufu

their mouthpieces
turned towards the gods

have disturbed
only the mud-brick
mastabas

DISCOVERY

The experience of commuting into London must surely have helped to persuade us that there were better things in life than lining the platform every morning like figures from the Papyrus of Anhai, changing on to the Tube and coming forth by day at Oxford Circus. A Monday to Friday of shuffling filing-cards in the shadow of the Post Office Tower at the expense of the BBC, then the same crowded route westbound home to Barnes left me sapped of all creative will, all intellectual curiosity, without even the time, money or energy to go to a play, a concert, a gallery, to take advantage of living at the heart of things. Married a year, with a nice little rented flat in a 'lion house' by the Thames, with a landlady who took the *Morning Star* concealed inside a copy of the *Daily Telegraph*, why weren't we content? The very ease and conformity of the life was stifling us. It was as if we were writing experimental entries for a modern *Book of the Dead* and becoming all but mummified in the process. Mummified, but not parentified. That was not even up for discussion. If anything, I feared that starting a family would stop me writing, and Jane was wary of the whole idea, conscious of the difficulties she had been through with her own parents and anyway she had no patience with little children. I didn't think of myself as adventurous – that spirit comes almost entirely from Jane, with her African colonial background – but once we came up with the idea of going abroad, there seemed to be so many possibilities. And once we heard that we would be sent to Upper Egypt (after the initial shock, assuming they would honour our request not to go to the Middle East) the research began. Even before we embarked on the VSO induction courses, we were wading through recommended volumes, pausing on the way to the South Bank beside Cleopatra's Needle, popping in to Sir John Soane's and making unwonted diversions to the British Museum. If we had known then just how precarious the VSO Egypt project was, we wouldn't have been so thorough. But the pleasure of discovery was well under way.

If you had asked me whether I was especially interested in Egypt before then, I would probably have said no. It took some time to register the steady drip-drip of incident and encounter in our lives that now makes my obsession seem what Hans Keller, my BBC boss, would have called 'ineluctable'. But I think I would at least have mentioned the opportunity I had in 1972 to see the visiting 'Treasures of Tutankhamun' at the British Museum. My German exchange partner, Jürgen, was with me that July and we queued for over three hours, although my diary notes that others between the barriers must have been there for six or seven. 'Great experience,' the bold, loopy scrawl goes on. 'But was it worth it?'. The entry is squeezed between a sentence about playing mini-golf in the park and one about buying some secondhand LPs, which gives some idea of my priorities. It was at that curious point after school is over but before A-Level results have come out. The future is on hold. UCCA, the old name for what is now the Universities and Colleges Admissions Service (UCAS), still sounds like one of the Egyptian gods and it certainly felt as though a higher force was in control. I didn't know as I queued that the discovery of the boy king is a story that has much to do with waiting, nor did I feel at the time any particular affinity with this other eighteen-year-old. Nevertheless, seeing 'Tutenkamen' (as I spelt the name) must have impressed me at some level and I realise now that I was lining up for something I hadn't quite clarified. If I had thought about it I might have seen a clue in those Ted Hughes poems I had been reading and the analogy between patiently waiting for a fish or a fox and seeing the page printed with magic. I returned to the occasion fifteen years later in the quasi sestina (which follows this chapter) whose obsessive form – six 'rhyme' words repeated in different patterns – was chosen to suggest the weaving of the queue.

You might expect a 60-year-old to feel more closely attuned to such things, but I had a similar experience at the B.M. only a year or two ago, pressing to get close enough to see their *Book of the Dead* exhibition of papyri, and feeling unexpectedly cool about it all. But it has to be said that at eighteen I was still more interested in making films and trying out conjuring tricks (mostly bought from Davenport's in the aptly named Coptic Street, right next to the museum) – something, incidentally, that seemed to appeal to the poet of fox and fish when I came to correspond with him in the late 1970s: 'Tell them you're a professional conjuror' he wrote, when I asked about how to get theatres to take my verse dramas – it would prove I was willing to throw myself into the 'battlefield', to stand up and improvise a show 'in peril of being laughed off'. But that there could be magic of any other kind than what was offered by Standard 8 film and TV conjuror David Nixon did not enter my consciousness any more than the suggestion that poetry was a battlefield.

I was slow to realise that Ted Hughes was a Prospero among poets, yet the encouraging letters he sent a year or so before we applied for VSO must have contributed to my decision. 'You have to live, I think, a bit uncomfortably', he would tell me, with a final reliance on what he called the 'survival energy' within my writing.

The actual tomb of Tutankhamun, when we eventually visited it, was something of a disappointment – like someone's living room, and utterly without atmosphere compared with other tombs in the Valley of the Kings. My chief memory of the visit is the security staff's amazement and disbelief that we didn't have a camera. Seeing the treasures again in Cairo was extraordinary, however, and it would not take much to persuade us whenever we were in town to scurry along to Tahrir Square to gaze at the gold mask – or, at least, one of the gold masks, as the innermost solid one was away on its world tour, a fact that Jane still laments. There is no image more compelling, even on a T-shirt or a tea towel, even reconstructed in the bizarrely situated Tutankhamun museum at Dorchester ('an unforgettable experience, spanning time itself. Two minutes walk from the car park'). And there is no story more enthralling. I could not find a way of telling it while we were actually living in Egypt, though I read everything I could about the discovery, including Howard Carter's own account of it. It was not until I came across a book by a former head of the Metropolitan Museum of Art in New York that I found a way in. *Tutankhamun, the Untold Story* sounds a rather sensational title, but it was a ground-breaking study by Thomas Hoving, which explained what really went on in the 1920s. The fact, for example, that Carter and Carnarvon were not heroically restrained as they claimed to have been: they entered the inner chamber the moment they had a chance, then concealed their act later. In one of the photographs you can see a reed basket leant conveniently against the wall concealing the hole they had made. Nor were they exactly accurate in their record-keeping. Several items disappeared and then turned up either with Carter or at Carnarvon's home in Highclere.

I liked the idea that whereas Carnarvon was one of the richest men of his day, Carter was from ordinary, unprivileged Norfolk stock. His grandfather had been the gamekeeper to Lady Amherst and the boy impressed the local gentry quite early on with his animal paintings. Young Howard only found his way into Egyptology because of this skill, which made him an invaluable draughtsman in days when photography was not really adequate for recording purposes. He first worked for Flinders Petrie in the 1890s, sketching the finds and murals and reliefs at various locations in Thebes, but notably Hatshepsut's palace at Deir el Bahri (one of the most striking of all the temples). Carter had risen to be inspector-general in the Egyptian Antiquities Department by the time he teamed up with Lord Carnarvon, initially on further excavations at Deir el Bahri. Tensions of class came into play in this relationship, but there were other differences too. Carnarvon was married, with a daughter, Evelyn, who took a keen interest in the dig. His Lordship provided the money, of course, though for all his wealth (spent largely on racing and fast cars) he did not envisage extending the funding beyond the fifth season in 1922. It was a time of inflation, there were extravagant rumours about just how much the Earl had sunk into the Valley (£25,000 it is estimated) and some people were muttering that he should look to the 36,000 acres he was responsible for at Highclere. Carnarvon was not a man to listen to mutterings. He had lived life, as we say these days, in the fast lane – a metaphor that needs, however, to find room for the wild elephant that chased and nearly killed him. Carter and Carnarvon were not the only ones interested in that particular part of the Valley at this time either. The American Theodore Davis, who had dug for twelve years and for whom Carter had worked in the past, only gave up the concession after some wrangling and prevarication. It was the discovery of some Tutankhamun seals on objects unearthed by Davis that gave Carter renewed hope for the final season. The American was convinced that he had already found – and indeed had published his account of finding – 'Touatankhamanou', just as he also believed he had located the tomb of Akhenaten, so there was no real fear.

Carter had a very thorough and systematic approach to his excavation, a method taken from grid layouts used in artillery barrages during the First World War. He divided up the relevant triangle of the valley floor – the only one they had not yet examined – into squares which would be explored carefully in turn. The work involved was colossal and relied entirely on manpower without any help from machines, just hand-tools and reed baskets to remove the thousands of tons of sand through each seven month season. The entrance would at last turn up very close to the entrance to the tomb of Rameses VI, which is two centuries older than Tutankhamun's. Carter had already noted back in 1917 the remains of ancient workmen's huts near this tomb, which should have been a good sign and encouraged him to look more closely in that vicinity, but curiously he did not follow up on this lead (perhaps wishing to avoid the tourists who flocked to it) and turned his attention to the opposite corner of the triangle. So years passed as he doggedly worked his fruitless way back to that original, hopeful spot, having to make encouraging noises for Carnarvon's visits, just occasionally able to stir up some excitement (Lady Carnarvon was able to handle thirteen alabaster jars they found). It was the men's water-boy who stumbled on the step that would reveal the sixteen steps that descended to an entrance and a cartouche with Tutankhamun's name on it. The only reason that this tomb was untouched was that it had been concealed by debris from years of flash floods. The boy found the step on a date which has always stayed with me, '4th November':

At home, the leaves
will by now have turned,
and the small boys

cart from doorstep
to foggy doorstep
masked pyjamas full

of the *Daily News*.
croaking 'Penny
for the Guy, guv?'

But here the sand
is already ablaze,
and that momentary

crackle under the
soul, that brief
flash from my boyhood,

is smothered by
this day's ambitions.
The morning is on

41

a blue fuse and
the men are
standing clear.

Silently they nod
to where a small boy
awaits me on the step

he has unearthed.
(Penny for a
Golden Rain, guv?)

All the various elements I have mentioned so far contributed to my 1991
book, *The Tutankhamun Variations*, whose construction probably owes
something to my stint at the BBC with Hans Keller, a friend of Benjamin
Britten (and dedicatee of his Third String Quartet). He had considered
Britten an essentially monothematic composer, for whom variation form
was the most natural and I had often felt that something similar could be
done in verse: a series of unexpected 'takes' on a single theme. As well as
including pieces like '4ᵗʰ November' written from a surprising perspective,
and more personal anecdotes such as 'The Treasures of Tutankhamun'
(see p. 45), I attempted to juxtapose details about the excavation with
other historical events – so, in one poem, tourists reminisce about their
picnic at the Somme trenches. And I interwove different styles of verse:
there were lyrics, narratives, monologues (a glimpse into Carter's psyche
as he dreams of 'folding doors/of intense gilt' or as he revisits the tomb in
1924 when there has been a dispute and the sarcophagus lid is suspended
over the masked mummy), together with all kinds of stylistic shifts as
when a Chorus of Reporters starts to intone:

We are looking for a story.
A running story, like the war.
But not the war.
An English story.
Like Jack the Ripper.
Like the Titanic.
Like Scott of the Antarctic...

Carnarvon had an exclusive contract with the *Times* – even today it is quick to publish any item about the Valley of the Kings – but the world's reporters were always looking for something to fill the gap left by the Armistice. That there was so much secrecy surrounding the dig only added to the frenzy, so when the Editor of the *Times* was spotted heading off to Newbury races (a racecourse very near Carnarvon's seat), and when Carnarvon himself cancelled all his engagements, there was mayhem. What really made the journalists foam at the mouth was any hint of a curse and soon there was more than a hint. The stories that have circulated since those days are wonderfully diverting but usually have little truth in them. However, it is true that Carnarvon did die soon after the tomb was opened – of an infected mosquito bite – and his favourite dog did howl back in England just at the moment he died.

My inclination is to stop writing now, dear reader, as a mosquito – the only one I have noticed in this wooden box I call my study – has literally just flown into my ear. I am pleased to say that I hear no howling dog, only an angry mosquito – but alas, even as I type those words, Jane has just brought me tea with the news that there was a strange black dog in the garden... Thus it is with stories about Tutankhamun. The rumours begin to fly, the superstitions begin to bubble. It is safest to leave the description of the opening to Carter himself, whose words I can never read without a thrill of excitement:

> Slowly, desperately slowly it seemed to us as we watched, the remains of passage debris that encumbered the lower part of the doorway were removed, until at last we had the whole door clear before us. The decisive moment had arrived. With trembling hands I made a tiny breach in the upper left-hand corner. Darkness and blank space, as far as an iron testing-rod could reach, showed that whatever lay beyond was empty, and not filled like the passage we had just cleared. Candle tests were applied as a precaution against possible foul gases, and then, widening the hole a little, I inserted the candle and peered in, Lord Carnarvon, Lady Evelyn and Callender standing anxiously beside me to hear the verdict. At first I could see nothing, the hot air escaping from the chamber causing the candle flame to flicker, but presently, as my eyes grew accustomed to the light, details of the room within emerged slowly from the mist,

strange animals, statues, and gold – everywhere the glint of gold. For the moment – an eternity it must have seemed to the others standing by – I was struck dumb with amazement, and when Lord Carnarvon, unable to stand the suspense any longer, inquired anxiously, 'Can you see anything?' it was all I could do to get out the words, 'Yes, wonderful things.' Then widening the hole a little further, so that we both could see, we inserted an electric torch.

It is a good metaphor for our arrival in Egypt. We too were at first 'dumb with amazement', we too would see 'wonderful things', we too would be blessed or cursed with the obsession and spend the rest of our lives cataloguing, as I am cataloguing here. Item, the toffee-texture of a single dried date from the *souk*. Item, one glass of juice made from freshly crushed strawberries. Item, the smell of water on the dust at 5 a.m. Item, a solitary locust on the corniche at Aswan. Item, a black kite snatching a sparrow from the balcony. Item, a tent with disconsolate soldiers on the edge of Atlas. Item, one home-made mosquito net. Item, a hibiscus flower. Item, a bunch of tiny bananas. Item, the trunkless pair of legs our neighbour saw walking the street below. Item, the taste of coffee in a bedouin's tent. Item, Asmi's freshly laundered cotton shirts against my skin. Item, a *muezzin* heard across the Nile. Item, some phrases of Arabic that glimmer and twinkle – as I step out of the shower (*hanneyan!*), as I rush to get my breakfast (*wahida wahida*), as I make a promise (*en'sha'allah*).

The Treasures of Tutankhamun
The British Museum, 1972

I am waiting, like all the others, waiting
to open the sacred seal and discover
my future; and as I wait, this exhibition
snakes me through steel barriers to my golden
eighteenth year where I catch, amid the darkness
that enfolds a teenage Pharaoh's history,

glimmerings of a more personal history,
as if it had lain beneath the sand waiting
for me to come and dig into its darkness
in search of the famous Mask but discover
only in each glass case my own face, golden.
It is my coming-of-age exhibition.

All aspects of me are in this exhibition:
the child's chair and board game are a history
of my early youth; my teens were that golden
dagger. This trumpet, this cow-bed are waiting
for me to experiment, to discover
in their cross-meshed passages of darkness,

in sexual unity and divine darkness,
the Goddess Hathor's milk-white exhibition
of her transfiguring powers: discover
between her lyriform horns all history.
The Necklace of the Rising Sun is waiting
to embrace us, its clasp is cool and golden...

Each morning my hopes shoot greener, but golden
futures only bloom after months in darkness,
during nights of counting the weeks of waiting,
and now at this jubilee exhibition
I am persuaded that time and history
are relative. Come, UCCA! and discover

to me the sacred light, let us discover
the place where we are to spend our golden
prime and inscribe our names on history
as one young man did, emerging from darkness
at eighteen to become this exhibition –
the very thing for which we are all waiting.

SURVIVING

We were at the High Dam by 8.30. No one had been certain about the departure time – or date – of the boat, so we arrived early prepared to sit it out, which is just what we had to do. It was 5 p.m. by the time the boat drew away. But it was a decent vessel, with half-decent toilets (not exactly clean, but 'plural' as Jane put it), though no other facilities except the services of a of an old tea-maker, partially blind, hunchbacked and squatting on the lower deck. That rather smelly but warmer area was taken over by the locals and their livestock while the fifty or so Australians, Americans, Europeans opted for the open upper deck where the views and the sun and the stars were. Our fellow upper-deckers were world-touring, easy-going types, with not much money but time to spare. We claimed a fine spot in the middle and piled our luggage around us, a great water container that it took two of us to carry, blankets, pillows, food for five or six days, a bucket on a rope (for washing), lots of warm clothes. There were five of us: Stuart, Alan, Jane, me and Martin from El Minya. Ahead lay 170 miles of uncharted, unpopulated lake.

The voyage was far more beautiful than any of us had anticipated, with islands everywhere – the tops of mountains, drowned beneath the lake. It was strange and somewhat disturbing to see that smooth expanse of blue, so flat and innocuous and to think that beneath it lay many temples no one would ever visit again and the sludgy remains of villages that twenty years ago were thriving settlements. It's difficult to convey the size of Lake Nasser, except by comparing it to the sea. On either bank at first it was desert, low, grey or yellow, rugged or undulating. Ahead was the faint divide between water and sky, barely distinguishable, one a slightly darker blue. As the hours passed so the terrain would modify itself, sometimes to quite substantial brown, gold, purple mountain ranges, then again to green, half-fertile skerries, closing in on us then parting again until we could have been on the high Atlantic. Except for the calm. There was little wind. Some wavelets. And a clear course to the south.

All in a hot and copper sky,
The bloody sun at noon,
Right up above the mast did stand,
No bigger than the moon.

We scanned anxiously for crocodiles, having been told the lake was full of them. Not one did we see, though there were quite a few seabirds and even what may have been an osprey near the shore. It's an unreal life, moving relentlessly down into Africa on an old boat, and Joseph Conrad would have recognised the tub we were on. Originally at the port we had found two large vessels lashed together, the one we were to inhabit, which was just a shell, with no engine, and another one with cabins, sundecks, lifeboat and suchlike. Fine, we thought, we can hop over there when we want a change of scene. But they took away the smart boat before we left and replaced it with what was no more than a tug, which they had lashed beside our shell. No complaints. The method seemed to work and there were many good nautical reasons why you shouldn't tow a boat. Meanwhile, eating was our main pastime: home-made meat loaf, which lasted the whole trip, twenty-four hard-boiled eggs, forty small loaves (though no miraculous fishes), six big loaves, two kilos of peanuts, four kilos of oranges, a huge tin of rice salad (which went bad very quickly because we put tomatoes in it), sweets, bananas, luncheonmeat, cheeses, dried dates, condensed milk and tea on request from the boat's 'cook', who once even gave us *ful* beans. When we weren't eating, we were reading, talking, playing cards and word games. The days seemed short because after sundown we couldn't do anything but get under blankets, chat, sing, sleep, or gaze at the stars, which were simply astounding. It wasn't really stars we were looking at, but galaxies. So far from any source of light pollution, the entire sky was a mass of jewels, constellations lost in the cosmic reach, though the Southern Cross could be picked out. There were meteors and passing satellites. It was a sight I shall never forget. But it was cold and didn't get warm till a good while after dawn. We resorted to whatever methods we could to retain heat (Jane slept with her legs in her cardigan). We should have brought sleeping bags – or tents, as some of the passengers had. It's remarkable how significant the sun becomes when you're exposed like that. Never had Akhenaten's religion seemed more understandable than as we lay begging the pink fuzz round a desert peak to burst into a yellow solar disc.

Arriving at Abu Simbel was rather an anticlimax. Having moored at what we took to be a little village south of the temple at 3 or so in the morning, we all went back to sleep and thought we'd have a leisurely start to a day of exploring. But at around 7 rumour spread that we were actually there and that the boat was leaving again at 10 sharp. Two days' travel for less than three hours at the temple? Much less, in fact, since it proved to be quite a hike to Abu Simbel. We had a rough idea of the route but didn't want to get lost as we'd heard horrible tales about deadly puff adders and sand scorpions. We made it in good time and – once we'd overtaken a Frenchman buying 127 Egyptian pounds' worth of tickets – found ourselves standing before the famous colossi, gigantic survivors of Nasser's great flood. As with the Pyramids, the first sight of any 'wonder' can be a letdown, but we gave ourselves ten minutes to grasp what we were seeing and its full grandeur began to sink in. Colossal is the word: the four statues of Rameses II are impossible to escape. Walk back a hundred metres and they're still as big, perhaps bigger, and when you shift your imagination into gear and visualise what they must have looked like before they were sawn into chunks, moved sixty-odd metres uphill and reconstructed by UNESCO, when they were part of the continuous line of cliffs rather than a hill perched on a low bank, then you find yourself feeling very small beside them. Although the original setting must have been splendid, now it's very beautiful on account of the lake and the curious desert beyond. I had never seen desert with that sort of appearance: pyramid-shaped mountains surrounded by perfectly flat yellow sands. Those sands covered most of the temple for many centuries. Flaubert was just one of several travellers to lend a hand clearing them in the nineteenth century (managing to 'disengage the chin of one of the the exterior colossi') and these 'stupendous monuments' came to feature among Baedeker's top recommendations. No doubt some of the atmosphere has vanished, that sense that a work of art has been standing in a certain place for thirty centuries, and it's tempered too by the knowledge that the sandstone has been injected with resin to make it easier to saw. What is remarkable is that even when the blocks were all fitted back together, the accuracy of the workmanship was such that the sun's rays at dawn still penetrate to the inner sanctuary. We looked inside and saw the well-known carvings of Rameses in his chariot, fighting accompanied by his lion, beating back Nubian slaves, all very violent and egotistical. We also had our Wizard of Oz moment and inspected the hollow dome of the artificial mountain they erected to support the salvaged temple. It's vast, like a James Bond film set, which perhaps sums up the aesthetic of much Egyptian sculpture: crowd-pleasing blockbusters from Middle Kingdom Studios.

We had a fine view of the temple as the boat set out again, dwindling to a postage stamp after an hour's chugging, then finally mingling with the other desert scenery. Before the sawing began in 1965, the figures must have looked from a distance like the natural rock. I don't know which is the more impressive in the end, the achievement of the pharaonic designers and workers or that of UNESCO's planners and engineers. One has to admire the motives of the 1960s team more. Has there ever been such an example of international co-operation? The space station, maybe? But in the case of Abu Simbel all that they had to show for it at the end was what had been there in the first place. It's Rameses who still gets the plaudits; no one remembers any of the names associated with the UNESCO project. Yet the job got done, which might well have been a lesson in democracy to certain Egyptian leaders in decades to come.

Now we were looking forward to a predictably lazy and uneventful voyage home. We were by this time familiar with the boat and with each other. A rhythm had been established on board and we were relaxed and rested. As far as I know, there were no albatrosses about. At 3 in the morning, we woke to find ourselves moored.

Day after day, day after day,
We stuck, nor breath nor motion;
As idle as a painted ship
Upon a painted ocean.

We assumed that the crew were resting and thought no more of it. We were told later that one or two people heard a strange bang, but also turned over and slept. I was one of the first awake, just as the sun was rising. The rest of the travellers were laid out like mummies in their sleeping bags. I looked through the railings behind my head and saw the crew wandering around at the back of the tug looking rather puzzled. The one we assumed to be the captain, a weak-looking old man with dapper white shoes and Nubian dress, stood waving his arms feebly and frowning at everyone. The engine was not running. We were in the middle of the broadest section of the lake with shoreline just visible, and it was windy and unusually choppy. The boats were swaying to a noticeable degree. Then I saw a Nubian crew-member strip to his shorts and hop in the freezing, churning water at the stern and come up with a frayed length of steel cable in his hand, the other end of which appeared to be attached to the tug. What had happened, we surmised by 7 o'clock, was that they had been towing us rather than driving us from alongside, and either the cable had snapped or else the two boats had come too close together and the cable got caught in the rudder and then the screw, thus stopping all motion. And now as the sun rose on a very cold and stormy Tuesday, the crew were trying to put the problem to rights. We weren't overly concerned, not even really when the waves started to shake the boats about in a way we hadn't realised was possible on a lake. And there still seemed good reason for Stuart to turn over and say he'd get up when we were moving again. They were obviously going to do something about this soon. We were in the middle of a virtually uninhabited lake on which there were only a couple of steamers a week and the odd fishing boat. Of course they were going to do something about the problem, because if they didn't we could be on that lake for days. Nobody back in Aswan would care. They wouldn't send out searchboats for a week at least. Well, we had enough food and there was 'water, water everywhere', all drinkable. Then there were all those fish... and crocodiles.

They seemed to be having difficulty with diving because of the swell and the whirlpools caused by the movement of the boats. So the worthy crew hauled the tug round to starboard and lashed the two boats firmly together to have another try. And as they were doing so, we had a good look at that boat. It was built in 1928 by an Egyptian firm. It had nothing. No flag, no siren, and needless to add no radio. This was, remember, pre-cellphone, but this vessel looked pre-historic. By the afternoon, the protective padding on its sides – tyres and rope – would be ripped off through incessant abrasion and its panels would be on the verge of giving way. But the crew, having tried to dive again and untangle the cable, gave up all hope and left us in the hands of Allah for four or five hours in increasingly heavy waters. What was most unnerving in the whole affair – more even than the captain's complete lack of initiative or concern, his shrug of 'Allah will make it simple' – was the hammering of the two boats against one another every few seconds with a spine-prickling, gut-wrenching boom from our hulls. We all looked on, clutching the rail as we were tipped over fifty or sixty degrees from right to left, hoping that someone who knew something about boats might take over in some way. But we were in the hands of Allah. Although there were a dozen things that the most simple-minded landlubber could have advised them to do, the crew would not take away that privilege from Allah. Admittedly, I was trusting that He was on our side, too, and we were all praying like anything, but I'm sure God likes to see His people helping themselves where they can. The culture clash was painfully audible and we feared the plates were about to come off.

By mid-afternoon, things were pretty serious, and the jokiest of us were worried. The two vessels were going to pull each other apart; if they weren't, it certainly looked and sounded that way. The conditions were dire. Worse still, we were creeping ever closer to some evil-looking mountain peaks just above the surface of the water. Yet it was comforting to be closer to land, having drifted that way for three or four hours, because we were by now thinking in terms of lifebelts and desperate swims – and crocodiles. But we knew very well that if we could prevent the boat from capsizing and keep ourselves off the rocks (Heaven knows how) we might stand some chance. The trouble was, the time. Once night came, that would be it. Jane describes it in a letter home:

> When the full horror of our position began to dawn on me, I did all the typical things like hoping it was a dream and that I should soon wake up and wondering if it was really me this was happening to – like a film, only happening to *me*. I prayed; I thought of our families and what the effect would be on them if the worst happened; I thought how unimportant were most of the things I usually bother about in comparison to just being *alive*; I wished and wished I could see into the future and know how it would end; I felt cold and sick with fear; I worried about John and the married years and children we would not have. I wondered if all the other passengers were thinking the same things as I and I cursed and bemoaned our helplessness in this situation.

She goes on to describe two of the worst moments, firstly when 'an elderly Australian woman sitting on my left leaned confidentially over and said 'Do you know how to take down and use a lifebelt? It probably won't come to that, but if it should…' and when she told me that the hefty young women opposite me had been a stewardess and was ready to 'take control' when the time came'. Secondly, she describes after four hours managing to stagger down to the toilet:

The loo not being the sort one sits on, but squats, it was a while before the ship was steady enough to obtain a balance; when I did I was terrified by a hideous crashing and banging overhead as though the whole edifice was about to collapse on my head and I was soaked by floods of water overflowing from the cistern on to my shoulders and back. I tottered out; and on the lower deck the Egyptians were huddled miserably under their blankets. Through the gap in the side of the ship I could see the tug pitching and bashing our boat, with the crew squatting helplessly on it. A row of silent Europeans sat along the edge of our boat watching it. I saw an Egyptian lift up some planks in the middle of our boat and look worriedly down and then call to some others. I went up and said 'Is there water down there?'. He said there was. 'A lot of water?' 'Yes, a lot.' I thought it was all up with us, and bent down to see into the hold. I could only see dry wood. 'I can't see it,' I said. Then the Egyptian laughed and said, 'No, there isn't any water.' A horrible joke!

Our only genuine hope was to spot a passing boat through the binoculars (thank God we brought them) and attract its attention. We were well off the usual route now and we knew anyway that the next ferry wasn't until Friday. Still, we stared and stared at the horizon, hoping. The last section of a long poem that I wrote after the event seems to capture something of the atmosphere:

the crew
pivot to Mecca

as the boats
pirouette

up
now down again

broad
hungry
the water

our Captain squat and still on the bows
his arms dangling
frowning at his white slippers

not a word

we're
huddled here
like infants

the shore
our classroom frieze

primary yellow
disney blue

But Coleridge is better:

At first it seemed a little speck,
And then it seemed a mist;
It moved and moved, and took at last
A certain shape, I wist.

Stuart had spotted some figures on the island we were very near to grounding ourselves on. We flashed a mirror at them and soon a rowing boat of fishermen had come out to see what was up. They desperately tried to tow the entire thing away from the rocks. There wasn't any hope in that. But meanwhile an Egyptian soldier had seen with his naked eye some craft way over by the west coast. A couple of miles off, maybe less. Through the glasses we could see what looked like a steamer and another boat. Action stations. Apathy had spread from the crew to our deck and it was impossible to stir the rest of our companions into action, to make them realise the seriousness of our situation (and even as I write this I recall several stories in the intervening years of multiple fatalities when ferries caught fire or capsized on Lake Nasser and the Nile). They all, I think, assumed that we were safely in the hands of radio, helicopter or lifeboat. This is Egypt, friends: don't expect it to be done for you, do it yourself. So we set to – some of us, anyhow – flashing mirrors and waving. I commandeered the lining of someone's large double sleeping bag – bright blue – and we waved that. Then I began shouting and soon everyone got the message. Alan bravely clambered on to the bows and swept a sheet through the air. In short, we made every human effort to attract the steamer's attention and they were some of the most tense minutes I have ever spent as we watched those vessels sailing in what seemed at one moment to be the same course, then the next a course towards us. We couldn't be sure. Certainly the big boat was going straight on along the shore and despite the shouts of 'He's coming!', he patently wasn't. But there was that blue speck, making a diagonal course across the lake. He could be coming our way. We waved, shouted, whistled, flashed. The crew even stirred themselves from their corpse-like resignation and someone actually thought to switch on the red night-lamp – quite invisible at that time of day, of course, but at least the thought was there. The tug, by this time, was nearly capsizing with every fresh wave that struck.

Thank God, thank Allah, the boat came. It was a fishing vessel, I think, a tug-like thing, but it didn't matter what it was like, it could save us. Cheers went up and yells of *Hamdillallah!* – Thank God! There was singing and leaping, kissing and hugging, we all breathed again, the booming of hulls sounded less like a death knell, colour returned to our cheeks and it suddenly became an adventure, a story to tell, something to put in the memoirs. We were towed to an island, where we stretched our wobbly legs, much to the horror of the crew, who told us there were snakes and scorpions there – and to prove it, one of them caught a scorpion, tied it to a thread, removed its sting and dangled it in front of us to frighten us. As if we needed frightening any more. Anyway, the Nubian divers worked well now that they were in shallow water and actually managed to disentangle the steel cable from the prop. We were perturbed to see our rescuers sail off into the blue leaving us to our Ancient Mariner and his crew of corpses, but when the engine started up and we'd been going a while we began to relax a little, although not entirely until we saw the High Dam's Tower of Friendship on the horizon.

And now, all in my own countree,
I stood on the firm land!
The Volunteer stepped forth from the boat
And scarcely he could stand.

57

Philae

When he went to pieces
she collected
the fragments and resurrected
(save a short
bit a crab had
gobbled) the god Osiris.

Greeks and Romans
worshipped her, but no man's
claws would ever court
her out of his coma.
No crisis –
river dammed
or temple drowned –
would surge her thoughts
from the dry sound
love made.
          Paralysis.
Bedridden. Blind
with wear. Yet behind
this confused water
clear sunk mind
observed the stasis
in her sanctuary
shattered, mystery
dismantled, the heart
removed from history

and Isis.

DAMS

The Upper Egyptian way of life has been dramatically affected by the construction of the High Dam. When we lived there it was easy to forget that only a generation earlier the annual inundation would have set the pattern for everything else in the year. Nasser's decision to do away with this time-honoured phenomenon was momentous. The attraction, of course, was electricity for all and the notion was generally welcomed by Egyptians, but it must have been alarming socially as well as politically. The waters of the Nile that make Egypt's existence possible run through other countries first. From before Nasser's day up until 2010 those 'source countries' honoured her historical rights to use that water. But just a year before the Arab Spring six of them signed an agreement challenging Egypt's prerogative and its traditional veto on any developments. Imagine the consternation that would be caused by an upstream damming project on the same scale as Nasser's... Imagine, indeed, what would have happened if Sudan or Ethiopia had built their own High Dam first. Before Nasser's big idea, the inundation was the true power in the land. If you knew that a flood was coming and welcomed it, you would naturally adapt accordingly. Left to its own devices, the Nile would have begun to rise at Aswan in June, reaching its highest point by September, crops originally being sown on to the freshly silted flats ready for a harvest in April or May. Decades of increasingly complex irrigation schemes (barrages, ponds, canals and devices such as the Archimedes screw, the *shaduf*, the *sakkiya* water wheel) helped conserve and redirect the country's most precious resource as they still do. But there wasn't much nostalgia for the inundation among the people we knew in Aswan, nor much evidence that it had ever happened – except for the Nilometer on the west bank.

This shaft for measuring the rise of the waters was constructed in Roman times, though it's probably on the site of an earlier one. We used to sit at the bottom of its steep sloping passage watching the world go by in feluccas. I even tried sketching it once, it was so compelling and mysterious. Shallow steps within the Nilometer lead down to the river and its stone walls are marked with scales to check the level, with inscriptions in Greek, Arabic and French. Although nowadays the minimal changes in flow are monitored by satellite, I imagine it was still checked by the locals as late as the 1950s, although not with quite the same concern – one of its prehistoric functions was to set the level of taxation: the higher the water, the higher the taxes. We visited the Nilometer a few times since it was situated on Elephantine Island, one of the local beauty spots, the oldest settlement in the vicinity of Syene (as Aswan used to be called). Unsurprisingly, the colonial British bagged the island as their base when they constructed the first dam and what is now its museum was once the home of Sir William Willcocks, architect of the old dam and one of the masterminds of Egypt's irrigation system. Whether it's still true I don't know, but he used to be the sole Englishman still commemorated by a street name in Cairo. An elderly man who worked on Elephantine Island showed us round the lush gardens of Willcocks's former home: mimosa, bougainvillea, lilies, jasmine – all of which he, of course, picked for the ladies in our party.

People forget the old English dam. It's the High Dam, a stone's throw up the Nile, that everyone goes out to see, but the original 1902 Aswan dam – rather looked down on by Egyptians – is a beautiful piece of work with its two kilometres of elegant granite buttressing like the octaves of a pink piano. The leafy settlement next to it became one of our favourite watering spots, the site of the old British community, Khazan, a green, civilized, gently decaying outpost with rather a Chekhovian melancholy to it and an Englishness (there were laburnums). The club we used to visit for special occasions such as our farewell to Alan and Stuart, in April 1980 was appealingly situated overlooking the dam and the braided course of the old First Cataract. To our right, Lake Nasser and the High Dam; to our left, the as yet unsullied islands curving round towards the distant tower of the Oberoi (now the Mövenpick), Aswan's ugliest hotel. Behind the club the chrome yellow dunes began. What a place to enjoy *bassboussa*, or 'kiss-kiss', that indulgent sickly sweet cake whose pronunciation the novelist Alaa Al Aswany makes a kind of shibboleth for sexiness (an emphasised s is good news, apparently). You could see why Sadat chose to come to Khazan every winter... or was it that Khazan had been preserved in all its colonial splendour because of its presidential appeal? I imagine he drew inspiration from the dam's power to hold back gathering forces of destruction. Sadat was certainly spoilt and protected from reality wherever he went, as no doubt was Mubarak after him, as no doubt are our own leaders. When he came to Aswan during our time, suddenly hundreds of trees appeared around the town; they were uprooted later, presumably to be planted in the next place he visited.

Soon after our own arrival in Aswan (no trees, no banners) we spent an afternoon near Khazan with our new friend Bhutros, clambering over the rocks below the dam, chewing sugar cane, singing and watching the sun set. Wild geese and other flocks of birds were heading down the valley, which is of such importance as a migration route. When we returned some weeks later, the same spot was engulfed in a roaring torrent. The sluices had suddenly been opened. A dramatic sight, but I'm glad I hadn't seen it when we were happily wandering at the foot of the sluice gates, and I like to think that Bhutros (who lived nearby) had inside knowledge of these things. During our second year we were given a closer look at the dam by a French engineer. He took us into a disused sluice right through the body of the dam and along beside the five-stage lock that was once regularly used to transport the Sudan ferry. We also saw where his company was building a small town for a hundred French families as part of a new project to construct another power station and as we walked through a pretty little village it soon became apparent that these people were going to lose their homes. The engineer shrugged. They knew what was coming, they would be compensated. By the time we left, all the tranquillity we associated with the English dam had been banished, and we didn't return.

The old dam was controversial from the start, as dams usually are, because it resulted in the the flooding of Philae Temple, the 'Pearl of Egypt', one of the fixed points on any Victorian traveller's itinerary, a pause after their shooting of the seven rapids of the First Cataract, which was a popular middle-class adventure at the time. Florence Nightingale's account of that particular experience is worth reading, how the boat is hauled between the whirlpools and the rocks:

> We approached the Fifth Rapid, and it seemed impossible that we could be going through that – the passage so narrow, the current so rapid, the rocks so sharp. We threw out two ropes, one on each side, for here our line of tactics altered: the rapid was too winding, the angles too numerous for us to pull to a stone; we had a line of men on each side to pull at us, and, of course, the fixed point wanting, the difficulty was greater. Crash went something: the right hand rope had broke, and the boat whirled round; but our bows caught upon the opposite rock. The other rope held, at which sixty men were pulling: the

'bigs' worked like heroes – in the water – out of the water [...] and we pulled through.

It's no wonder Florence Nightingale became the woman she did. Whether Jane and I should ever have had the courage to undergo this trip if the Cataract were not beneath several metres of water, who knows? It certainly put our Abu Simbel adventure in perspective. Philae, the temple of Isis, was the next major recovery project after Abu Simbel. Like Rameses's temple, this one would also be sawn into pieces (the analogy with Osiris's dissection is irresistible) and reassembled on a different island. There was a grand fundraising operation which included proceeds from the 1972 Tutankhamun exhibition at the British Museum. Photographs of Philae lined the route the queue had to follow. I was in that queue, although I had no idea at the time that I would come to know the place so well before the decade was out. Until UNESCO swung into action this enchanting monument was semi-submerged for much of the year and the rest of the time coated in sludge. The High Dam would have left it almost entirely lost under water and subject to scouring tides. 29-year-old Florence Nightingale anticipated her visit as 'a great day – the day we touch the Holy Isle, the day of Philœ [*sic*]....What a poem, for him who could imagine it!'

Well, as it happens...

Philae, half submerged beneath the rising waters
of cold war and engineering and power. No longer the preserve
of pale watercolourists from the nineteenth century, not since

the English dammed it to its annual inundation before
the First War, not since the Russians started an uprising
to overthrow it after the Second. Yet a mad whim

on the west wind suggested: *cut it into many pieces,*
as once Osiris was cut, then let these lotus flower
buds that strain above the flow of blue silt open

and blossom again. Isis's words? UNESCO heard
and her sacred boat there on the tide-marked wall now floats
in its proper element: her sun and its horns at last free

of nudging carp, Nile monitors, the teeth and cubic
tonnage of crocodile lamentation. The single obelisk
not in a Dorset garden has begun to write on an African sky

its sequel to *The Book of the Dead*, a tale of its own deciphering,
how imprisoned Flower of the Rose is released by Nile creatures
to meet her love, the island flourishing into renewed belief

that here is the source, that all beyond is a Land of Ghosts,
that this is the promised page, the thousand and second night
that keeps a doomed soul alive through its swirling narratives.

The last few lines of this recent poem not only refer to the belief that the
source of the Nile was actually at the First Cataract, but draw on one of
the tales from the *Thousand and One Nights* (a title which in Arabic – *alf
leila wa. leila* – sounds delicious) set in Philae. Zahr el-Ward ('Flower
of the Rose') was in love with the king's son and so secretly imprisoned
in the temple. When he at last tracked her down, the waters around
Isis Island were crocodile-infested and he only managed to make the
crossing when one of the beasts took pity and gave him a lift. Since so
many of the stories associated with this area are about pent-up passions
and frustrated consummations, the dams at Aswan begin to have a
symbolic as well as a practical significance. Safe at last from the ravages
of hydro-electric power, the removed and reconstructed temple of Isis
was officially reopened on the Island of Agilkia when we were living in
Aswan, in March 1980. There was even a special concert in the Palace
of Culture to celebrate. The Egyptian Conservatoire Orchestra played
– for political reasons no doubt – French, Russian and Egyptian works.
Men and women were performing side by side, we noted, which must
have been an affront to Upper Egyptian mores. Most of the audience
were audibly amused at the sight of a young German waving his arms
about on the podium, and there wasn't a great deal of concentration.
Five rows of plush red seats had been installed in the front row for all
the dignitaries, who were brought complimentary Pepsi during the
Tchaikovsky. The hissing of a hundred ring-pull cans was, I suppose, no
worse than cannon and mortar effects.

Our own visits to Philae could be magical. That wasn't the case on the chaotic school trip when we were also meant to be taking the kids to Kalabasha, another rescued temple, but ran out of time and I became thoroughly enraged. Nor was there much fairy-dust when we had an altercation with boatmen because they would not be reasonable about their prices (they have a monopoly at Philae). And, of course, there was the occasion that Jane was pinched by a passing young man and gave chase, shrieking Arabic denunciations, while our guests from England looked on in bewildered admiration. Even without such episodes, any visitor has to put to the back of their mind the ravaging of the site by European bounty hunters. There is only one obelisk now; its companion can be seen (as in my poem) on the lawns of Kingston Lacey House, Dorset, which is at least a change from the Thames Embankment or the Place de la Concorde. Approached in the right state of mind, though, there is nowhere like Philae: the bas-reliefs are incomparable. I have returned there in imagination repeatedly, trying to capture something of its poetry.

Our expert on the other dam, the one that would produce all that power for sugar processing (and for the chemical fertilizer plants which only became necessary because there was now no silt) was our friend Gamal, whose own life is a story of concealed pressures, not least because we suspected him of being a member of the secret police. Gamal was quite a lonely character and was keen – too keen, it soon became clear – to be our friend. Most of the men we knew would not feel comfortable talking to Jane alone, but Gamal didn't seem to mind. Perhaps this was because of his personal circumstances. He was recently divorced but had no choice but to go on living in a small flat with his wife, children and ageing mother. Divorce under Muslim law is easy enough: you just say 'I divorce you' three times to your wife. Finding somewhere else to live thereafter is not so easy, which is probably why he was forever descending on us. Gamal used to work on the High Dam and was a great enthusiast for its benefits, preaching the undeniable advantages of the three harvests a year it made possible and explaining how it was insurance against famine because it regulated the Nile's flow and stored water for lean years. He had some unsettling anecdotes for us about the life there: 'The High Dam was like the war, you expected to die...' he told us. 'One night in 1964, two thousand men died when a stray dynamite detonated... I was there next morning in the same position ... The lorries had taken the bodies away, the boxes were made and the bodies were sent with a thousand pounds and a handshake back to evicted Nubian families... Nothing was said. No one knew how many.'

One day in May, Jane and I were determined to take Stuart for a swim among the islands near the old dam. He had almost reached the end of his two-year stint and this (along with the drink at Khazan) seemed to be a fittingly memorable finale. Jane had come to know these islands quite well through her friendship with a Russian botanist who was working on them and described seeing sensitive plants (the ones that close up when you touch them) and a species of thorn supposed to be the one used at the crucifixion of Christ. She played down the snake tracks. And we didn't talk about bilharzia, the pervasive blood disease spread by snails in the muddy fringes of the river. But we were all determined to swim It was to be a pleasant little escape from the crowds and the dust. Gamal appeared just as we were setting off and he wanted to sweep us out to some grim chemical plant, which didn't really appeal in the summer heat. When we told him that we planned to swim, he said he would accompany us, but he knew as we did that in *Sa'idi* society it wouldn't do for him to be seen in the company of scantily clad Westerners. A letter of mine from that day in May continues the story:

We were glad we set off so early because the day was cool and easy to walk in. We found a *hantour* this end of the souk and it rattled us along the corniche, up the hill past the Cataract hotels then down a litle side road towards the Nile. We were after a Nubian named Abdu who is the man the university gets to row lecturers about on their various research projects. Needless to say, we soon had a crowd of villagers around us once we dismounted from the 'carriage' and paid off the driver, but a small boy was dispatched to fetch the boatman in question. We stood around on the quay looking up towards the English dam. Abdu wasn't available in fact, so we were rowed by his wife or daughter, a jolly Nubian lady, swathed of course in her black *milayeh*. Although we'd planned to go to one of the smaller islands nearer the dam, she was only willing to ferry us across to 'Dance' Island and because it looked a bit muddy around the fringes, we didn't think we'd be able to swim safely. Still, we disembarked and started walking through thick grass, among verdant foliage. All kinds of reeds grow around the islands, long-stemmed giant grasses and leafy green tubular things, and Jane pointed out the shrub associated with the Crown of Thorns. The thorns were very vicious and the tree has rather attractive yellow flowers, which the locals pick and feed to their donkeys. The island is uninhabited but some people go there to cultivate what we presume to be *ful* beans and maybe *bersim*, the clover they feed to their livestock.

All the islands of the First Cataract are granite, but there are intrusions of various other igneous rocks, making the terrain fascinating to walk over. What's more, since the dam has stopped the inundation, a large area of the island we were on showed the effects of prolonged exposure to Nile water: holes and smoothed curves, a glassy polished appearance, the course of the river now dried up into an impressive little canyon and everywhere pebbles and tiny shells. Above the water level you can find hunks of pink granite left by the pharaonic stone masons, the chippings still lying where they fell some thousands of years ago, the slots still in the off-cuts where they'd intended to insert wedges and dampen them so they would swell and split the rock. We wandered around these areas for quite a while, enjoying the solitude and the rich atmosphere of the place.

The highlight was when we at last found ourselves a cove at the southern tip of the island, sheltered from the view of anyone on the banks and offering a broad expanse of gently flowing Nile water with rocks and promontories to climb on to or swim around. Jane was first in, delighted with the spot, and I soon followed. It was quite easy to plunge from the edge because it was all granite rocks and the water became deep pretty quickly. Swimming was bliss! You had to be careful not to do yourself a mischief on the hidden rocks (we all sustained grazes) but apart from that it was as safe as a swimming pool and infinitely more beautiful. The water was not cold at all; in fact, we were more troubled by a light, cool wind that sprang up than by the water itself, but of course by half-nine the sun was making itself felt.

There follows an extended meditation on the likelihood of our contracting bilharzia ('80% of people have it here') which can hardly have reassured our families.

The more vivid recurring fear in my mind at the time, however, was what would happen if the High Dam were breached. It doesn't take much imagination to see what an attractive target it was for a terrorist from 1979-1981 and the dam was always bristling with soldiers. Egypt was much despised by its Arab neighbours after the accord with Israel. The destructive power of ten pent-up inundations is appalling enough to contemplate. Today, almost half a century from its opening, with allegiances and alliances crumbling throughout the region, the effects of such an attack would dwarf the Boxing Day tsunami.

HEP

The belly dancer in the Oberoi Hotel
gleams like a Nile perch glimpsed
beneath the erotic flow.

Upstream, old Willcocks still holds
back the waters of the Mountains of the Moon,
but on this islet

the sluices are open: Pernod after Pernod
with a French construction engineer from the new
hydro-electric plant.

It is the hips generate, water turning white
to kick us into life. Afterwards
returning across the Nile

feeling the pulse of each high-voltage
gyration in the tension of no common language
and the taut lateen sail.

Egyptian Mysteries

That the island where we swam was called Dance Island I had long forgotten when I wrote 'HEP' fourteen years later, but it seems appropriate. In a society where so much is culturally proscribed, where men and women have to keep their distance from each other, dancing is a useful pressure valve. There was, of course, the dancing for tourists such as I describe in the poem. There was the publicly acceptable Nubian folk dancing that you could pay to see most evenings in the Palace of Culture and which no Egyptian would have any problem enjoying. Jane was even asked to record the English translations of the announcements for this event, and for all I know they are still playing them. Then there was the other, bizarre yet apparently equally normal dancing at weddings, where men knotted a scarf around their hips and gyrated provocatively to other men. And there was the dancing shown on the tomb walls.

There is no doubt that a powerful erotic current runs through Egyptian society, channelled between oriental instincts confined by Islamic and Coptic mores on the one side and by pharaonic hedonism on the other. I certainly felt that some of the statues in the dusty old Cairo Museum carried an unmistakeable sexual charge and the very innocence and restraint of Egyptian women could be disconcerting – probably even more so now that the hijab is commonly worn. So much in society seemed designed to tantalize. The temples themselves, drawing one deeper and deeper towards an inner sanctum, appeared to be dropping veils, and the reliefs on the walls with their phalluses and nubile dancers were not exactly from the puritan school of art. If all this had such an effect on this Westerner, it was images from the Western media that burrowed their way into Egyptian men's eyes, like the bilharzia worm. How else to explain the prodding and pinching Jane experienced as a matter of course when we were out walking? She became very adept at dealing with this, the most powerful deterrent being a few words in Arabic spoken very loudly – usually something involving *haram*. Shame is a potent force in Upper Egypt. Young men seemed incapable of separating the goddesses they had seen on the big outdoor screens from the woman they saw next to them on the bus or train. Pinching was perhaps not so much a sexual approach as a way of finding out if this was flesh and blood. I must confess that sometimes the Egyptian reliefs and statues had the opposite effect on me: is this really stone? I suspect that the internet and satellite TV have not contributed much to the position of women in Upper Egypt – although I read not long ago that a female television celebrity was thinking of running for president.

Curiously, Omm Sety moved seamlessly from the world of cinema to that of Ancient Egyptian deities. Dorothy Eady (1904-1981) was born in Blackheath and her father, who was then a tailor, would eventually run a 3,500-seater picture-house in Plymouth. By the time we were in Egypt she had long been a fixture at the site of Abydos, north of Qena, the most sacred site in the country, home to the Mysteries of Osiris. Her story is hard to credit, but we met people in Egypt who had met her so we knew (without pinching) she was flesh and blood. The full story is told in Jonathan Cott's *The Search for Omm Sety*, but essentially after falling down the stairs at the age of three she came to believe that her real home was far from twentieth-century London. Through visions and recurring dreams the idea took root that she had in a former life been a temple priestess and consort to Pharaoh Sety I. Having sensed that Upper Egypt was her true home (this came upon her when she saw some photographs of Abydos in a magazine) she would not be satisfied until she had made her way out there. Nor indeed until she had found an Egyptian to marry ('I had been carrying the torch for King Sety since I was fourteen years old and was always hoping to meet someone like *him*') and a way into archaeological circles, which her obsessive studies soon made her more than fit to join. Her domestic incompetence, however, and her bizarre, unlady-like behaviour eventually drove her husband away; but the visions of Abydos and of Sety became more and more pressing, involving specific locations and very specific intimacies. To cut a long story short, she set up home near Abydos with a reputation, a menagerie and a clutch of friends, and became a tourist attraction in her own right as well as the foremost authority on the temple. It is said that when she first arrived at Abydos she astonished the resident archaeologists by knowing far more about the site than they did, and pointing them in the direction of things they had not yet discovered, but which she had visualised.

What emerges from the story of Omm Sety is what often emerges from tales of the occult: a little sex, a little psychology, and a big mysterious black hole. We did visit the Temple of Abydos, which is situated on the spot where Osiris's head is supposed to have been buried

74

by wicked Seth, but I remember little of the occasion except looking down into the waterlogged Osirion, a cenotaph which was one of the focal points for the Mysteries of Osiris, and associated with what Nagel's Guide calls 'certain conceptions of cosmogony in which the world was believed to have emerged from a primal ocean'. I think we had barely heard of Omm Sety at the time. It was certainly long after we had left Egypt – at about the same period as I wrote 'HEP' – that I published my long poem *Omm Sety*, constructing it to represent the structure of the Osirion, with equivalent numbers of stanzas to pillars and so forth. The book-length narrative juxtaposes imagined speech by the Pharaoh with passages about Omm Sety and glimpses of our own time in Egypt. On the face of it it is one of the most arcane things I have ever written, yet it is one of the few poems that people have come up to me and enthused about – women in particular, so perhaps I was tapping in to something of the Isis myth again. The stanzas at the end of the chapter will suggest the kind of work it is and show how I have, for example, used the shape of Osiris's still unexplained 'djed' pillar in the layout of the narrative sections, and how Sety's own words (in rhymed italics) pay a final tribute to his beloved.

If Omm Sety's mysteries were rather more profound than ours, nevertheless they had cats in common. In our second year we acquired a very Egyptian-looking black-and-white kitten, and once we had overcome the problem of how to stop her getting ringworm (the treatment for which is scratched on my soul) and realised that it was folly to let her out of the flat, she was good company. We called her Mitzu, vaguely remembering a cat by that name in Yeats. In fact, we were confusing the Irish poet with a Japanese electronics manufacturer. Minnaloushe was what we had been straining for, but Mitzu she remained. Then one day she disappeared. We had shut her on our balcony to stop her using the guest bedroom as a toilet and a couple of hours later, having forgotten I'd left her there, I went to release her and she was nowhere to be seen. It seemed impossible that the little scrap could have jumped from such a height, although there was a car parked underneath which would have made it not quite so unthinkable. We looked high and low and as luck would have it that night was virtually the only occasion that it rained when we were in Aswan. It was positively wet, bleak and depressing as an autumn evening in England. The area she could have vanished into was pretty bleak, too, full of rubbish and rocks, drains and stagnant pools, wild dogs and surprisingly sleek full-grown cats who thrived on the waste fishbones from our rest-house. There was no sign of her. We had a torch we brought out from England, but it didn't help us find her, nor did any of our cries of *Mitzu, Mitzu...* So we gave her up for lost and persuaded ourselves that she'd be better off with others of her species and that she'd survive happily because of all the rubbish nearby.

Two days later Jane was standing on the balcony and calling the cat's name again, desultorily looking through the binoculars to where the fat cats gather at sundown (I was listening to the Mendelssohn Violin Concerto in our bedroom) when she thought she heard a plaintive mewing. She called me to listen and it did indeed sound like Mitzu – but where was she? Every time we called she answered, but whether she was above, below or beside was impossible to determine. Jane dashed out to search while I hung over the balcony and we compared notes. Jane said up, I said down, so it must be somewhere in-between. I hurried to collect Yussef (one of our porters) and we tried to track her down. At first we thought she must have somehow got on to one of the other balconies and was shut in a flat, but as I bent beside the car below our window the mewing grew louder – and when I thrust my hand between the chassis and the front wheel I felt the soft (somewhat skinnier, somewhat dirtier) form of little Mitzu. Whether or not she had been there the whole two days, we don't know, although she didn't seem ravenously hungry. She was pleased to see us, though reacted badly to being washed again as she was every day during the ringworm crisis. We had no children in those days, so the protective instinct must have been very strong. Losing track of our first daughter in Totnes when she was a toddler must rank rather higher in whatever the emotional equivalent is of a Nilometer. We didn't have another cat until we had two daughters, in fact, and we called this one Ziggy, not after David Bowie but because of the cat's graveyard near Zagazig, sacred to the feline goddess Bastat. She was and still is our little Bastat.

Cats are peculiarly Egyptian. There is a terrific statue – one of a whole cache Belzoni found in Karnak – of the lion goddess Sekhmet sculpted in black granite. I still have a photograph of Margaret Thatcher standing before one with my typed caption: *Sekhmet the Destroyer*. A souvenir of the 1980s. But it is the Sphinx at Giza that most people visualise when they use the word and it has become muddled in our minds with the one that challenged Oedipus. It didn't make a huge impression on us when we saw it that day at the Pyramids, but I do have a very vivid memory of walking up a long avenue of smaller sphinxes towards Karnak. I find I also have a few sphinx-like individuals lingering at the back of my mind. There was a girl who appeared in our lives towards the end of our stay, a Circassian, of royal lineage apparently, whose every move broke Upper Egyptian convention. And there was the other prize-winner at the Alexandria Poetry Festival, trapped in an unhappy marriage and mewing to the bleak night from behind her medal's hubcap. Both of these women were utter mysteries to me. In fact, Egyptian sphinxes are invariably male – and I think of our dear friend Ahmed, a large generous man whose face, however, was inscrutable, or Hassan our Nubian friend ever searching for the second volume of Dr Johnson's *Lives of the Poets* or on a silent trek towards some remote semantic oasis.

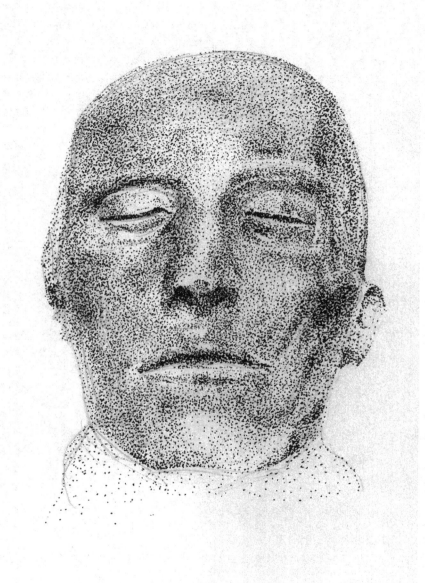

from **Omm Sety**

We
were packing all our souvenirs and gifts
for the flight back home
when you set out on your voyage to Amenti,
Omm Sety. We had stayed
two years, our poorest and our richest,
you – half a century
of intercourse across thirty centuries.
Scent or strain of music,
gesture, profile, touch,
that last glance back –
like paintings in the Tomb of
the Remainder of our Lives, just one
false door, marked
POETRY, to allow the *ka*
to come and go as now
it does, remembering that day
in 'eighty-one, when –
did we even hear about it? We were too busy
arranging who would take our cat, a note
in our diary says she was very nervous, it was
'an odd evening'. We said goodbye to our friends
resting our eyes again on the West Bank.

Leave your cats, your Teti-Sheri,
your Hor-em-heb: on this last ferry
no Rameses, Ankhsi, Ahmes, Mery.
Your animals will sing to you.
Leave your gander, leave your goose,
Snofru, Nebet, set them loose.
You need no watch on your new house.
Your animals will sing to you.
Leave your rabbit, leave your dog
Khalouli. Surely leave that frog
called Pharaoh to his monologue.
Your animals will sing to you.
Leave your birds, your peregrine.
Like these vipers, shed your skin.
My horse Mut-ho-tep calls you in.
Your animals all sing to you.

                We
        who love her, find a mysterious life
              in Abydos: other ears
    than mine have heard the music in the halls,
          the sistrum, tambourine and pipe.
      And other eyes have seen the golden glow
             in the Sanctuary of Osiris
    when no lamp was lit. And I have stood
              alone in Pega-the-gap
            at the Great Feast of Osiris
            listening to the jackals howl
            but at midnight, immediately
            the jackals were hushed, a deep
            silence fell and I
            felt myself surrounded
            by a great multitude of people,
            heard their breath, their feet
            on the sand, and as I passed
    through the gates of the Temple of Osiris,
    their presence, their breathing, their whispering feet
    vanished into the past, and I was left
    with only the stars and the cold of ruined
    walls, their clear impenetrable text.

EGYPTIAN IMAGES

While I have written obsessively about Egypt, I don't dream about it, which is a surprise, as I dream regularly and vividly. In fact, I tend to have the kind of dreams that would have interested the Biblical Pharaoh. There was the night I saw my father floating down among the stars in something like a coffin. It was the night he died. On another occasion, I was woken by a dream of R.S. Thomas so vivid that I fetched a book of his poems to read. I heard on the radio next morning that he was dead. My dreams are forever being 'broken' as they intersect with some coincidental fact in ordinary life.

More enjoyably, I frequently find myself in conversation with artists – recently with Samuel Palmer, for some reason, and then Robert Graves last week. But no one from Egypt. It could be that the imagery of that time has become so much a part of my conscious world, that it doesn't need to lurk in the dark. By writing repeatedly about the country and its culture I am, as it were, feeding the beast. I think of the Serapeum, that terrifying labyrinth near the step pyramid at Saqqara. I've never been back there in my dreams. Never approached that abandoned bull sarcophagus, left jutting at an angle, blocking the dark passageway, where it was dragged two and a half millennia ago. Or you might expect that I would wake up sweating with fear at being shipwrecked on a snake-infested island in Lake Nasser. Or find myself zig-zagging the mountain roads in a crowded taxi out of Edfu. At the very least, futilely shout in my sleep, 'What's your name?' to sixty blank faces in a hell-fire classroom: what teacher isn't always having teaching nightmares? But not about Egypt. No, my dreams remain as they are, their landscapes mainly English pastoral, at best faintly Italianate. I walk footpaths, I climb mountains. Most frequently they take me back to the area around Heathrow where I grew up, a terrain which, when I was still a student, I tried to Egyptianise by turning the Tube journey of one 'Namssenisub' (a cunning inversion of 'Businessman') into a progression through the stations of the underworld. When writing *Heath*, a book of poems about the area in collaboration with Penelope Shuttle published in 2016, I was astonished to discover that on the site of the old HMV buildings, where I used to work:

                    they found a statue
from the second century BC, Egyptian, of a priest
carrying the shrine of a god
                                    as if he had picked out
a boxed set of the complete recordings of every mass
for the dead ever written from Beethoven to Berlioz to Britten

I sometimes feel as if everything in my waking life is the dream and that, if anything, Egypt is dreaming me.

The difficulty in writing about the past is distinguishing imagery of genuine experience from mental reproductions of the pictures taken at the time. My father, when he visited, brought his Standard 8 cine camera, and the reel still exists even if the technology to show it has gone. One or two guests had sophisticated 35mm SLRs. We had an Instamatic, the very simplest and cheapest of pre-digital cameras, loaded by cartridge and without an in-built flash. For indoor photography, for shots of tomb walls or museum displays, for weddings or school events, we used 'magicubes', little clear plastic boxes which had a flash-bulb in a reflector on all four sides. We had to anticipate how many of these we might use in the year and saved them for special shots. The same was true of the films we brought out, which I think included a dozen or at most twenty-four pictures at a time. A far cry from the average modern memory card. Nor was there any opportunity to preview, select or delete: what you clicked you were stuck with. And then the developing... The only films we could get done locally were black and white. All others we sent back in the luggage of visitors so we didn't get to see what we'd captured until we were back in England. We were lucky and all our films made it home safely, but some of our friends lost their shots of the Valley of the Kings in an airport mix-up.

I didn't take many photos myself. I vaunted, like Miss Prism in *The Importance of Being Earnest*, that memory is the diary we carry around with us – but there are some in the albums Jane put together that, had Facebook existed in 1980, would surely have been prominent. There are, for example, several distinct photographic moments mentioned in a letter I wrote during our visit to the temple of Dendera, which we visited when we were attending a wedding near Qena:

We found ourselves walking down a very English lane, past fields, trees, and distant mountains. On all sides there were fellahin working in the fields. We were cheeky enough to take a photo of a man drawing a plough with two buffalo and he objected furiously (taking pictures brings the 'evil eye') then demanded *baksheesh*. Moustafa had accompanied us to Dendera because he lived nearby. You can imagine the palaver it caused when we turned up at his village, everyone pouring out to see us. He lives in quite a good house there with his mother and six brothers and their respective families. His father died some years ago. We gradually met everyone and were ushered in for tea. The prize belongings were proudly put on display – an alarm clock that didn't work, a cassette recorder that did and, astonishingly, a brand new electric fan. How much that represents to a fellah you can imagine, although I suspect it may have been owned by the village as a whole. We were offered fresh clotted cream, which we declined, and forced down sweet Sicola ('sickly cola' as we call it) for half an hour or so, whisking away hordes of flies. The family were loath to let us go without food but we consoled them by taking photos on our Instamatic: first one of all the men, then of all the women, because that's the way they seemed to want it. And thereafter a procession moved away from the village, like something out of a travel book. As we were leaving – the crowning glory – one villager stopped on his donkey to give us a load of fresh bananas, so Moustafa suggested that Jane might like to ride. She readily accepted and had a lift all the way back to the main road.

What we didn't preserve on our Instamatic was any shot of the interior of the temple, which is full of intriguing imagery, although I know what young Florence Nightingale meant when she said she had never seen anything 'so magnificent nor so vulgar... the work of some upstart *nouveau riche*.' To begin with, the smug Hathor faces on the capitals of the pillars make you feel as if you're under surveillance, but everywhere there are notable reliefs. Most famously there is – or was, before Napoleon's team spirited it off to the Louvre – the Zodiac in one of the chapels of Osiris. It is the oldest and indeed the only complete illustration of how the sky appeared to Egyptian eyes and imaginations around 50 BC and the one on which all subsequent maps were based. The Zodiac is circular, which might not seem surprising except that most Egyptian calendars – and there is a good example in the same chapel at Dendera – were rectangular. The original has been replaced with a rather poor reproduction, but through the gloom the animal iconography in the central area is recognisable: Taurus the bull, Scorpio the scorpion... On the perimeter are thirty-six deities each representing ten days of the ancient year. All this is supported by a ring of crouching falcon-headed male figures and the four bare-breasted 'pillars of the sky', physically contorted yet managing to remain dignified as they raise their arms in that posture so well known to schoolchildren. Schoolchildren might well be fascinated by the so-called Dendera Light, which we barely noticed, but which today keeps the internet chatrooms busy. It is a wall relief of pharaonic slaves apparently carrying what looks like a giant lightbulb. Not a low energy lightbulb (they weren't that advanced) but one with a filament. The conspiracy theories were as predictable as finding a face in the dust of Mars. So *that*'s why there is never any trace of soot in the tombs... The truth is that it's another example of wacky iconography: a symbolic backbone and a lotus flower spawning a snake. In fact, it looks more like a cucumber than anything else.

None of this did we photograph. Or even draw, although I frequently turned to my sketchbook, sometimes using pencil, preferring pen and ink, as my grandfather had – and as my daughter Rosie has for her illustrations here. I still have a dismally shaded, two-dimensional pencil sketch of Horus, the falcon god, from the temple at Edfu, which I would be embarrassed to show either of my daughters, both of whom have inherited Grandpa's superb natural draughtsmanship. The pen and ink sketches are better, I think. One I made of the Nilometer has gone missing (submerged by the flood of possessions) but there are two tolerable pieces on my study wall: in sepia ink, they are simple Nile-edge scenes, one with fellahin attending to what look like fishing boats, the other of grasses, a passing wildfowl and a distant cliff. But for capturing the moment during those two years, the device of choice was poetry.

We had come to Egypt after a year of marriage and five years of searching – Howard Carter-like – for poetic gold. It was in my third year at Swansea, where Jane and I met, that it dawned on me that this was what I wanted to do and during a year in Mannheim and another in Exeter, I familiarised myself with the canon, filled in those gaps left by my somewhat patchy undergraduate studies. Everything now centred on that obsessive determination to find The Poem. I tried to make a living as a children's conjuror which would leave me time to write, but I was never good enough, and always too conscious that conjuring was a deception. I was looking for real magic. When we got married I took clerical work at the New Music Department of the BBC which I knew wouldn't impinge on my creativity. I had half an idea to fund the poetry by writing TV or radio plays. But so much of what I was doing at this time was barely formed and I still hadn't written more than two or three poems that were anything like mature work. Egypt changed all that.

I was an Imagist in those years. When eventually *Westerners* appeared, Michael Hulse in the *TLS* compared the poems to early Ezra Pound and I had certainly done my time with *Hugh Selwyn Mauberley* and the *Cantos*. I remember also being entranced by Pound's versions of Confucius that I found in Alexandria (I have just taken that same battered copy down from my shelf and it has the Cairo British Council Library 'cancelled' stamp). When we were in Aswan, I was under the spell of the American doctor-poet William Carlos Williams and much of what I wrote in those early months has that long, thin prescription-pad appearance. Williams was a busy man, and wrote on the hoof. I saw the appeal of that. I was less interested at first in rhyme and metre, more concerned to listen to the language, to capture the image, to preserve the moment (though R&M kept returning after I started re-reading Louis MacNeice and wrote 'The Crack'). I think that Imagism is an effective way of filtering experience, which is why it works so well in Hilda Doolittle (H.D.)'s poems of the Blitz and why T.S.Eliot employed it in *The Waste Land* – a work much studied and quoted, we found, by earnest Egyptian students ('*walls of mud-crack-éd houses*' etc.). In The Black Land we were in danger of being overwhelmed by strangeness and exoticism. The answer was to narrow everything down, stare hard at one thing, keep it all under control and (as Basil Bunting advised) cut out as much as I dared. The poems that began to emerge were entirely new, but felt genuine, and I quickly realised that I had found my voice, that Aswan was my First Cataract, my true beginning. This notion of a source has since come to fascinate me, not least because Jane was brought up on the other side of Africa where so many trips to the source of the Nile began (she actually lived in Dr Livingstone's house) and we hope one day to explore those lands of her childhood, her own beginnings, a simpler time. But at this time, it was the image and the immediate moment that mattered.

At first I found it difficult to write about such raw experience, and my notebooks and the few surviving foolscap carbons reveal half-finished poems about everyday things. Only a handful – and some of those are here – would I wish to preserve. The best of them looked obliquely at our experience as Westerners in modern Egypt through the imagery of the past and in particular a set I called 'Museum Pieces', which took as their starting point some brilliant black-and-white photographs in a 1970 catalogue of *Treasures of Egyptian Art from the Cairo Museum* (Thames & Hudson). What was to become in effect a source-book was given to me by Alan and Stuart for my 26th birthday, and leafing through it now I see all the statues whose names became titles of poems in *Westerners*: 'Diorite Statue of Chepren (Khaef-Re)', 'The Wife of Nakht-Min', and 'Tuthmosis III', which was a piece I would later have to recite in Alexandria. I'm surprised now that they let me, since it's openly satirical of despots, but Mrs Sadat didn't say anything, perhaps remembering her own allegiance to Shelley who despised tyranny (that 'sneer of cold disdain'). Anyhow, the sun went on setting in the Mediterranean behind the half-imagined image of the Pharos as I read to the television cameras lines about 'the Napoleon of the Eighteenth Dynasty ... a pigmy imprisoned in greywacke' and his rivalry with Hatshepsut. I learned later, to my irritation, that greywacke has an audible final 'e' which rather spoils the music (it happened with 'stele' in another poem). In fact, I knew no more about Tuthmosis and Hatshepsut then than I do now and it's a general romanticised image of the period and of tensions within tyrannical regimes that I was trying to capture. The angry syllables of 'Hatshepsut' seduced my ear along with the potent dark stoniness of the sculpted greywack(é). This is 'Tuthmosis III':

in life
the Napoleon
of the Eighteenth Dynasty

its dazzling bull
victorious
on battlefields

in Syria
Mesopotamia
and beyond...

here
a pigmy

imprisoned
in greywacke

a perfect little
black curiosity

his nose
raised
like a hammer

Hatshepsut
he grimaces

the cobra
curling
from his brain

Hatshepsut...

he grips the staves
and hatred
blows across
the shallow eyes

Hatshepsut!

shivering
the royal beard
from its smooth chin

Joseph Campbell called dreams private myths, but so are poems. Of the publicly celebrated images from Ancient Egypt, there are some that haunt me more than others. Prime among these is the face of Akhenaten and his is a story that I have returned to repeatedly, from the early 'Amenophis IV Addresses the Theban Priesthood' , which had to be cut from *Westerners*, to 'The Amarna Stelae' (2004, see p. 180) and very recently my version of Akhenaten's 'Hymn to the Sun', a work I have been trying to translate since we left. Of course, Akhenaten has intrigued many artists, from Agatha Christie, who wrote a play (*Akhnaton*) about him in 1937, to Philip Glass, whose phenomenal minimalist opera *Akhnaten* was premiered just three years after our return from Egypt.

Tel-el-Amarna was the city established by the heretic pharaoh (originally known as Amenophis IV) when he broke off relations with the priesthood at Thebes. In founding the first monotheistic religion worshipping the Aten or sun-disc, Akhenaten, as he called himself, also inspired a radical new imagery. What little remains of Amarna – a remote location which Jane and I deeply regret not visiting – shows carvings of an intimacy and fidelity to truth (to 'Maat' as it was called) that are intensely moving. Just as Cromwell asked to be painted 'warts and all', so Akhenaten must have insisted that his court artists be faithful to what they saw, even if it represented a kind of sickness, or was unpharaonic behaviour, such as dandling babies or leaning out of a window to chat to passers-by – the equivalent, perhaps, of the British royal family's first walkabout. The latest theory is that the Pharaoh and some of his family were blind, explaining the highly tactile nature of the murals. Always as part of these family scenes the long straight-ruled arms of the sun's rays reach down with tender fingers to caress them and bless them. It's religious at the same time as it is sensual. But Akhenaten and his family suffered from a genetic condition that not only probably affected their eyesight, but made their faces and bodies look peculiar, like aliens almost, with long features and strangely shaped bodies. 'Now look at the/face of the man in the moon', I wrote in that early poem, 'at a cat's eyes/ at a nose long and ridiculous//as it meets these protuberant lips/with a snub //and my hips/that are round//like a woman's'. Even Nefertiti, the heretic's consort who was very likely a relative, bears something of this quality, yet somehow in her case it becomes beautiful. Hers is another image that haunts me, but in this I am hardly unique. The very name Nefertiti translates as 'the beautiful woman has come' and the (sadly one-eyed) bust in the Berlin State Museum has become as iconic an image of long-necked feminine beauty as the Venus de Milo or Mona Lisa. One of the poems I composed in Egypt that has endured the winds and sands of time most convincingly (it follows this chapter) is about Nefertiti's relationship with Akhenaten. At some point during their reign she took herself off to a 'castle in the north', perhaps because of his co-regent, Smenkhare. We tend to forget that Tutankhamun descends directly from this line and was most probably, if DNA tests are to be believed, Akhenaten's son, later forced to change from Tutankhaten to the acknowledge the 'hidden one', Amon.

However disillusioning our visit to the tomb was, I do not take much persuading to read a new book or watch the latest documentary on the boy king. My father was very interested in Tutankhamun and bought the widely-circulated Penguin account of the discovery of the tomb some years before the exhibition appeared at the British Museum. In my own Tutankhamun book there is a long poem 'For My Father', which tells the story of what happened when I took my parents to the Valley of the Kings. What it doesn't tell, because I didn't know until after the book appeared, is that when my father sailed to Iceland as a wireless operator during the Second World War, he went on a ship called the *Champollion*. Not only is Champollion, of course, the name of the man who cracked the hieroglyphs by using the Rosetta stone, but the ship named after him was the very same vessel that took Howard Carter to Egypt for his final season of digging. My father noted the lines in my poem 'Carter Begins': 'Aboard the *Champollion*, steaming/ towards the Pharos, unknown, unrecognised,//I imagine steps that lead into chambers/full of the poetry of this rock language.' He wrote to me remarking on the coincidence. The ship must have been requisitioned by the military, but he particularly remembered it because it was such a dreadfully unseaworthy tub.

To the Valley of the Kings, then, and the most distressing image that stays with me from our Egypt years: of my father lying beside a drainage ditch in a field of sugar cane, sinking deeper into a hypoglycaemic reaction. He had been a diabetic since the 1950s and he was the age I am now when he and my mother came out to Egypt to visit us. I had taken great pains to make it the holiday of a lifetime for them. My letters home from that period are full of instructions (some, admittedly, about things they should bring us, such as decent tea-bags and a hundred sticks of chalk). But at Luxor, where we met up with them, it seemed a good idea for them to do what we had done and cycle to see the tombs on the West Bank. It was a cooler time of year and the trip was perfectly manageable for 50-somethings. Unfortunately, my father had had a stomach upset and I think this must have affected the balance of his insulin and sugar, which was brittle at the best of times. As we were passing the ancient tomb-robbers' village of El-Gurnah, still inhabited, still no doubt concealing secret passages and forbidden goods, he was suddenly overcome, staggered from his bike and collapsed (with such irony) among the sugar. In the summer of 1987, I told the story using something approaching blank verse, having left my imagism on another shore. Too long to reproduce in full here, the poem addresses my father directly and culminates in the arrival of a stranger from that 'tomb-robbing Gurnah clan ... who climbed out of his taxi/and silently removed you to his house,/no rock chamber in the foothills, no cache/ of Middle Kingdom murals, but a simple/white-washed tunnel-vaulted house of mud brick/there on the fertile plain.'

If I had known then about the coincidence with Champollion, I would surely have incorporated it.

Nefertiti in the North

Not to be closer
to the roots
of this rose

in lands
where they say the Nile
no longer flows

but falls
like the sunlight

not to be watching
the bird-catchers
crouch
where the gardens end
outside my window

and that same figure
on my wall

not for the paintings
of his nets and his dog
driving from the papyrus thickets
a slim-necked waterfowl

not for these

and not to be quenched
by the sight
of the sand's disregard
for his sacred boundaries

never to scoff in triumph

'the-beautiful-woman-has-come'
has come

but since the King
is in the south
in the company
of his dear Smenkhare

I have come
to this castle in the north

CRACKS

Whatever led to Sadat's dramatic public assassination in 1981, the immediate installing of Mubarak kept a lid on the potential chaos and the sarcophagus remained sealed for another thirty years. When riots broke out in Cairo at the beginning of 2011, the full extent of the problems in Egyptian society that had been brewing for decades became apparent to the rest of the world. The cracks were there during our stay, but they were largely invisible to Jane and me, not only because of our naivety, though we were naive. No, it was also because Aswan is anything but typical Egypt. And even more because we were, as 'guests in the country', protected from much of what was happening, and our Arabic was never good enough to filter out (like sieving little stones from Aswani rice) the hard truths from the cosy welcomings.. Nobody in our community would have dared openly condemn Sadat anyway, except by suggesting that he was not a match for the god Nasser. There were too many snoopers, secret policemen, and besides there was a general feeling that peace was to be welcomed, even if there was private anger that Egypt had 'sold out' to Israel and to the Americans. But certain things that we took for granted were going to be the root of what would happen after the Arab Spring: the numbers of young soldiers who had returned from war and had nothing to do, uselessly guarding institutions, the dams, the power stations, the factories; the tensions involving both Muslim and Christian fundamentalists, which were becoming more than just anecdotal; the severe social difficulties – managing to earn enough to get married and find somewhere to live, managing to make ends meet on ridiculous incomes; the corruption, from small things at school to backhanders in the biggest institutions. There had been voices within the Arab world warning that something was going to give, but the West was slow to take notice and felt generally content to let Mubarak come down hard on troublemakers. We had heard rumours about police brutality, but we did not ask questions. As long as there was stability at the top, there was a greater chance of stability in the Middle East.

Looking at video footage from the events of 2011 in Cairo, metaphors of dams and cracks and floods come to mind, but also of glass partitions being smashed, the 'have-nots' trying to break through to the 'haves'. Although London has had its own riots, I cannot help but wonder how even the most deprived young people in Britain would cope with the kind of poverty prevalent in North Africa. I think also of those little ushabti figures that the pharaohs made sure were buried alongside them, figurines of servants so that they would have someone nearby to do their work for them in the afterlife (see the poem on p. 108). It's an analogy that I found myself making not only in the behaviour of some of the expatriate Europeans we met, who seemed to assume that they were entitled to the same privileges that were granted them in colonial days, but between classes of Egyptian. In late twentieth-century Egypt, the ushabtis had begun to breed in sufficient numbers to stage a break-out. 75% of the population were under 35 and they were strong. Tarek Osman, whose *Egypt on the Brink* foresaw much of what occurred, has since attributed the uprising (writing for opendemocracy. net) to 'a changing class structure, a decline in the regime's legitimacy, eroding institutions, the absence of a meaningful national narrative and a dramatic demographic shift'.

An immediate casualty was the Museum of Egyptian Antiquities, which stands right on Tahrir Square, one of the busiest intersections in the city of twenty million and the focal point for the revolution. When it was built in 1902, the attractive red neoclassical building had been in a quiet corner of Cairo. Suddenly it found itself at the epicentre of change. Images on YouTube show the aftermath of rioters streaming into the museum, smashing glass cases, turfing out mummies and reducing priceless prehistoric artefacts to fragments. By the time order was restored, seventy items were listed as damaged or disturbed (two mummy skulls were retrieved from the grounds) and eighteen had disappeared including the image of Tutankhamun with a harpoon. Its companion piece, a gold-painted wooden statuette of the boy-king riding on the back of a leopard (some say a jaguar), had been left broken beside its smashed glass case. It's an odd piece to fall casualty as it is still something of a mystery to Egyptologists, but as a symbol for the survival of high art in the face of prowling predatory forces, it will serve admirably. To see art wantonly destroyed is disturbing, although curiously there is almost an expectation that the most renowned antiquities will be maimed or cracked or damaged. So the Venus de Milo or the Acropolis or Nefertiti's bust take much of their potency from their semi-ruined state, which emphasises the fragility and so the miraculousness of such workmanship's survival. Think of the bust of Memnon that the Italian strongman and bounty hunter Belzoni brought back to the British Museum. It is one of the best known faces in that building, a huge granite fragment of a colossus, with an almighty crack across its torso. It is a natural geological feature in fact, but the crack gives it its legitimacy. The haughty, indifferent smile on its features gazes out defying time to do its worst. It was one of the inspirations for Shelley's sonnet on the transitory nature of all creative work, and the illusory nature of political power, but his cynical interpretation is not the only way of looking at the image.

The museum on Tahrir Square was one of our favourite haunts whenever we were in Cairo and several of my 'Museum Pieces' were finalised during visits. I remember standing in front of 'The Wife of Nakht-Min', for example, and scribbling lines that became a poem for *Westerners*:

His fat hands waggle, the policeman laughs,
and the loafing attendant licks the feather-duster handle.
All grease the glass with their noses, all pass the case
and take a snap. But some glance a second longer.

Her face, mutilated for reasons we don't know,
is still sufficiently fine to make us wonder
what else she hid behind the huge coiffure
fastened there like a cask of wine four thousand years.

Though the eyes and the lips have been destroyed
and a carved gold band is clamping the skull
so the plaited and tressed triumphal pylons
chain her in hair from head to chest,

she can still gaze and smile undamaged
through the small favours her sculptor bestowed:
a lotus flower opening under claw-tight buds;
pomegranates tucked beneath a barren strip of gold;

how the sheaved and stately queen comes firm and small
into a ripe young girl where the corkscrew curls run out;
how the severed hand that should have reached towards the king's son,
though severed, still clutches at some carved frippery;

and how an inspiration – the film of pleated
fine linen – ripples through indurated stone
to reveal the shapely abdomen and nubile curves
light, below the weight of a wifely crown.

> *my lover*
> *I like to go to the lake with you*
> *and wash there*
> *allowing you to see me*
> *wet*
> *in my linen gown*
> *of pure white*

There were others that never made it into print. Very often, as I have implied, it was the incomplete or damaged works that seemed to me most appealing. The Egyptian Museum wasn't always an easy place to go round: it was hot and airless, extremely crowded in season, and rather chaotically laid out. My notes from the time describe 'shambling, peering, yawning' between 'mini-skirts, polyester prints, hot pants, mummy-cloth, persea bouquets and an ostrich feather fan', observing 'airtickets being fingered before reconstructed chariots and chocolate bars being unwrapped in front of sealed sarcophagi' while a 'chrome-plated vacuum cleaner' glided among the Tutankhamun treasures. Having latched on to the Westerners paradox (in Ancient Egypt they were the dead), this kind of witty juxtaposition became my default poetic style, as did the superior dismissal of 'tours, tours, and curiosity smothered by the dust of a week', but I recognise the truth in the feeling I noted of finding 'yourself between your eyes and the object' – not merely because of all the glass.

2011 was hardly the first year in history that Egyptian treasures had been plundered. Even Carter and Carnarvon appear to have made a 'pocket collection' of pieces, some of which turned up at Highclere House. In one of my poems in *The Tutankhamun Variations*, I focus on a moment when cracks appear in Carter's own facade as he betrays an embarrassed fondness for two tiny gold coffins 'containing unborn/and unidentified babies,/ mummified and motherless' and purloins 'that lotus head,/cute and irresistible/as a first-born'. The most notorious thefts in the history of Egyptology had come before 1922, however, when dealers began to notice a surge in high quality artefacts on the market in the late nineteenth century. They were coming from the so-called Royal Cache, a tomb which was known to families in Gurnah beside the Valley of the Kings and which they were privately raiding. Events surrounding this story are captured brilliantly in Shadi Abdel Salam's 1969 film *The Night of Counting the Years*, which the volunteers were shown as part of the preparation before we left for Egypt and which I still find profoundly haunting. It all took place at a time of unrest not dissimilar to what we see now in Egypt and the location of the cache was only revealed because members of the family concerned were tortured and imprisoned by Daud Pasha. He released them into the care of the elders of Gurnah on condition that they surrendered the treasure. The source proved to be along what is today known as the Agatha Christie Path, a precipitous short cut to the Valley of the Kings, which in fact predates the existence of any of the tombs, although inscriptions along the route show that it was used by priests as a lookout across the Nile when they were expecting a pharaonic visit. John Romer in his book about the Valley describes the area vividly, 'the steep sides cut off from all sound... lonely but strangely hospitable'. Inside this complex of cliffs and clefts, which is only just south of the great outcrop into which Deir el Bahri temple is cut, is a crack in a sheer rock face, a 'chimney' some 150 feet high. Within the crack there is a shaft – itself cracked and crazed – which dropped forty feet down to a corridor and a painted coffin, then three more, and as Romer describes it, beyond a corridor 'strewn with numberless antiquities' was a seventeen-foot square chamber 'piled high with more coffins', their inscriptions 'like a roll-call of New Kingdom history'. The famous scene in the film shows the subsequent removal of the white-draped coffins in procession across the desert to wailing music and keening villagers. I still shiver to think of it.

In the light of thirty years, the great fissure in our own lives was opening up back in England and we did not realise. Jane's mother was not getting any better and there was an increasing gap between reality and fantasy in her letters. I hope it is not true that the final break came when we decided to delay our return by a few weeks when I heard I had won the Alexandria prize. If we had not gone, would she have then decided to come and meet us at the airport? Or might we have decided to go back to Jane's house first, rather than going to my parents as we did? As it was, we went to Alexandria and I read, along with the Tuthmosis poem, a piece I had written in Dante's *terza rima*. I had the rolling triple-rhyming metre in my head having just read the entirety of Louis MacNeice's *Autumn Sequel*. It is another example of a poem which only fell into place when I made a bold cut. It was originally half a dozen lines longer, but I took my poet's chisel and struck. It is a poem about the crack that made the greatest impression on me when we were living in Aswan: the one in the unfinished obelisk in the granite quarries. I have already described something of the atmosphere of this spot, but here I try to imagine what the reaction of the Pharaoh would have been if he had arrived one day in Aswan – or Syene as it would have been – expecting to see how his latest obelisk was getting on. He had ordered that it should be the biggest anyone had ever made. In the light of what I have been saying about tensions between different classes, this narrative should perhaps have the final word...

The Crack

The Pharaoh has arrived in Aswan today:
being cheered off the barge, being greeted
by officials from the quarry, on his way

through the streets, luxuriously seated
in a palanquin, to supervise the long-planned
raising up of his newly completed

obelisk. Across desert, up the grand
triumphal causeway carved for this occasion,
he's escorted to where the workmen stand,

their faces smooth, as if the abrasion
of a fear, of a persistent nightmare,
had ground them away. Without expression,

they watch their foreman whisper in an ear
and the quarry official gasp, fall dumb
and helpless and leave the foreman to steer

the guest away. He knows the worst must come,
but he can patch time, pointing out the vast
unyielding rock face and outlining some

of the problems caused by having to work fast
and make crucial cuts too quickly, with risk
of ruin... Leading the falcon eye past

the hollow of a previous obelisk
which only the rock's good temper had meant
it was finished and erected in weeks...

But the Pharaoh has begun his ascent:
lifted over the rock these men wrestled
to overthrow, shaded from rays they spent

long months exposed to – some of them pressing
the wooden wedges in the hard-worked slots
and dampening them to swell, some dressing

the hacked-out shape for the final cuts –
and all, even through the pink rock-dust, pale
as alabaster now, aware of what's

made out to quarry employees who fail
to finish their allotted task before
the Pharaoh comes. Today, it's a fairy tale.

But that day it was as if the earth's core
had pumped a deep black vein of evil up
out through the granite slab, and the men saw

the crack, as if they were watching a heart stop.

DECODING

ADMIRATION of anything in someone's house is likely to end up with you taking it home. You have put the 'evil eye' on it.

BECKONING is provocative unless you turn your hand palm downwards and use all your fingers. The most useful gesture is three fingers and thumb gently tugging an imaginary light-cord: *be patient.* If you are a man, never sit tapping your fingers together in front of another man.

CLASPING your wrist is also a bad idea.

DISCUSSIONS seldom go straight to the point, but include much conversational foreplay, polite circumlocution in which there will be extensive use of the many expressions of welcome in Arabic and much invocation of Allah.

ENSHA'ALLAH, 'God Willing', is an expression which punctuates all conversation and a nightmare for translators of Arabic literature ('If we're spared?', 'Hopefully...?', 'Fingers crossed...?') Any discussion of a future event must be put in the hands of God.

FLOWERS are picked wherever they grow, and men share them freely with each other as they walk hand in hand.

GIFTS are ignored, set aside, but they are showered on you as a guest, and GUESTS are honoured above all things.

HENNA nights – as opposed to Hen nights – are what the bride and her friends have before a wedding.

I AM cannot be said in Arabic because there is no verb to be. How, then does Hamlet manage?

JOHN is my name, therefore I am known as Mr John. Jane is Mrs Jane. We were particularly welcomed in a family where every member through all the generations had a name beginning with J.

KISSING seldom happens (in public) between members of the opposite sex.

LITTER is flung freely and left to the herds of goats to devour.

MUMMIES and temples and tombs hold little interest for many Egyptians: 'just some stones' as one of them said.

NOISE is the medium in which Egyptians exist, particularly at weddings.

OFFERS are made liberally – even marriage offers – but frequently offers to fetch unlikely things from far-flung places.

PRAYING in public is perfectly normal, sometimes on a portable mat, often with just a sheet of newspaper. Sadly, peeing in public is equally common.

QUEUING is a custom unknown.

RULES OF THE ROAD might as well be the Mysteries of Osiris.

SOLES OF THE FEET are offensive, so the American manner of crossing legs can look like an insult – as can throwing a shoe at George W. Bush. Car drivers hang images of feet (and evil eyes) to ward off tail-gaters.

TRAVELLING means hanging on to whatever bit of the bus or train you can reach, inside or out.

ULULATION is that shrill war-whoop of joy heard at weddings.

VERY is usually translated as 'too': 'I am too happy to see you!'

WAITING is a skill that Egypt teaches.

eXcept when it was just a hole in the ground, the most common kind of toilet featured the primitive bidet device we came to know as a turd-catcher.

YES means no and NO is the polite word for yes.

ZIP is not polite.

Ushabti

we are guests in a tomb
with that familiar mean muzzle

who will stretch himself and his bones
over any gilded chest   guard

with his cudgel tail
in his black coat
ears alert like bayonets

a culture
in unguents

the entrails of the Lords
Carnarvon, Cromer, Kitchener...

we are guests
in a tomb

where there are ushabtis
for every day of the year

and the lady of the house
has given us one

fragile in faience
its name faint

a statuette
of the kind excavators kick
to get at the sealed bonanza

we are learning how to speak
to our ushabti
thus:

O ushabti

should I be requested
to do hard work
of the kind
that has to be done
down there

instead of it always being me
who sows the fields
fills the water-courses
and carries the sand from east to west

you do it
you do it for me

husband
killed
in 67

four times a week
forty pounds a month
three children
one room
the other side of Cairo
she pushes
on to the two-piastre bus

only the days
the lady of the house
is getting her hair done
horse-riding
or rehearsing *Iolanthe*

can she work
in time

today she can't keep up

she pushes
till she pushes

(crack
and wel-wel-eh!)

    'the antique marble ashtray
    they gave me
    when I went to Barcelona'
off
    'the inlaid table
    they chose for me
    in Dar'
on to
    'the handmade carpet
    they presented me with
    before I came from Abadan'

ash
from umpteen
ambassadorial do's

    'irreplaceable –
    it's the sentimental –'

crack
and wel-wel-eh

horned
bifocals
wind sideways

venomous
dentures flash

   'there are two crates of duty-free
   in the boot –
   bring them up for me!'

and the ushabti answers
here I am
here I am
I will do it

POSSESSION

At any tourist site there would invariably be someone trying to sell us an ushabti. The poem that prefaces this chapter uses one as the basis for a satirical portrait of an excessively acquisitive post-colonial Westerner of the kind I hope we did not become. The very nature of ancient Egyptian burial practices means that there has long been a market for reproductions of such artefacts, generally more tat than Tut – not surprisingly in a culture which forbids any copying of the human form. The 'corniche' in Aswan is a promenade with a facade of souvenir shops designed to keep the tour groups happy for an hour or two. When we lived in the town there was no international airport and tourists were mainly those who arrived on a cruise ship, but also those who had flown in for a quick trip on a felucca, a drink at Agatha Christie's Cataract Hotel, a shufty at the newly opened Philae Temple and the High Dam then a flight on to the reconstructed Abu Simbel. We were rather scornful of the area at first, preferring the *souk* which ran behind it, but as time went by we became quite friendly with the proprietor of one of the gift shops, and ended up buying several bits and pieces from them during our stay. It was always a pleasure to go to the Philae Bazaar and have an idle browse while sipping hot sweet tea. I still have one of their little paper bags advertising GIFTS, ORIENTAL CURIOSITIES, CROCODIL & SNACK SKINS. Jane was presented with a flask of jasmine water during one visit; it's in our bathroom cabinet, only half used, and the scent remains powerfully evocative.

We did not think of ourselves as acquisitive. Yet the study where I am writing this (a worryingly coffin-like structure in the garden of our terraced cottage) is littered with paraphernalia from our Egypt days, some of it from the Philae Bazaar, but much of it received as gifts. Books are another matter. As I survey the stack of volumes about Egypt I can only be grateful that technology eventually moved on from the papyrus scroll. Nevertheless, we have somehow acquired a fair amount of papyrus too, occasionally stuffed in among the books (ironically), or hidden behind the furniture, in a frayed and crumpled state. Papyrus doesn't grow naturally in Upper Egypt, but there are specially cultivated plantations in the north, one of which I believe we visited with our Russian botanist friend, Ira, and it has become one of the most popular tourist purchases. Our best example of a papyrus painting belonged to my parents, who had it expensively framed, but it's spoilt by a ballpoint signature (this was my father getting over-enthusiastic in the gift shop and rather oddly persuading the bewildered proprietor to put his name to it). It's a mere possession, and I should really dispose of it. But there is one papyrus which possesses me, because it led to my poetry's first appearance on printed paper, and comes from the home of one of the world's greatest libraries. It hangs in a double-glazed frame in our living room, and it was handed to me by Mrs Sadat on the site of the Pharos in Alexandria along with a brassy medal which shows the blazing lighthouse (one of the ancient wonders of the ancient world) surrounded by a laurel wreath. On the back is an Arabic inscription and the words: ALEXANDRIA POETRY PRIZE.

As if the four thousand books weren't guide enough into any possible afterlife, I seem to have made myself a veritable burial chamber with so many pointless Egyptian grave-goods. Why do I hang on to that metal coffee-pot, for example, etched with a drunken sphinx and the inevitable pair of pyramids? Who even gave us that strange censer (one of our Coptic Christian friends?) or this blue pottery scarab? And why? For one or two of the pieces, I know precisely why.

Just behind my computer screen are the remains of a camel-bone carving of what looks to be a pharaoh. It is hard to tell, but the figure holds a lotus flower in front and there is something that must be the crown of Lower and Upper Egypt on its head. The unsightly blobs of Bostik show where I twice tried to repair this grotesque object, because it was a gift from one of my classes at Tagribeya girls' school, where I taught in our first year. William Morris would not approve, but I cling on to it. It's evidence that I was once a *modaris*, that I taught (though the security forces might not like to hear it) in a *madra'sa* – which is merely the Arabic word for a school. I had done very little teaching by the time I found myself standing in front of several dozen eager head-scarfed, trouser-suited Egyptian girls. That I barely knew any Arabic in the first weeks other than the vital instructions – be quiet, sit down, get out – must have been a marked handicap. Or was it an advantage that I could not hear what the pupils were saying about me? The noise in my lessons was unbelievable, the '*MISTER! MISTER! MISTER! ANA! ANA! ANA!*' ('ME! ME! ME!') and the constant craving for personal attention, for reassurance – 'Very good, Mister?' I must have been doing something right, even if it doesn't feel like it looking back. I know that my all-English, no-Arabic methods involved much pointing at things and a huge amount of repetition. ('DO YOU HAVE *BEANS* FOR BREAKFAST?') There was much learning of songs, chanting key phrases, endless question-and-answer, role-playing, guessing games, pronunciation games (is it *big* or *pig*? – to Egyptian ears the consonants sound the same) and competitions. There were occasional slide-shows, too, with shots of a typical day in suburban Middlesex, which caused much delight ('Your father is beautiful!'). And the cartoons I drew to elicit responses they seemed to enjoy. Even more, they enjoyed hearing me try out my colloquial Arabic. This was hazardous, of course, and there was the example of a volunteer teacher who had been trying to teach his class what a zip fastener was. In the end he simply pointed to the zip on his trousers and repeated the word to his class, who were falling about. Zip is Arabic for penis.

I have to remind myself as I sit in my comfortable study how basic the conditions were, even in a school which was considered one of the best (more rural schools I visited would have no electricity or running water): if there was a blackboard, it would just be painted on the wall and the chalk was more like cheese; if there were windows they were without glass, sparrows flying in and out during lessons, trains trundling and hooting past; and there could be up to sixty pupils in a class, crammed on to uncomfortable, often broken, benches. I would forever be telling kids to sit down, but who could blame them wanting to stand? It could be horribly hot for much of the year, although the school day was shortened accordingly as March advanced. But school could be very cold too. And the distractions... such as my birthday when there was an oriental dance performed to 'Happy Birthday' and a flurry of cards ('Good morning Mr John, everyyears you fine', 'How are you Mr John, I hop you many happy new year, bubi!'). Or the occasion when a weird keening sound floated across the desert towards us – the wailing, upward-swooping notes of mourning women, dressed all in white (or am I imagining that?) in a passing funeral cortege.

So I will keep the broken lotus flower figure. But what about that fly-whisk by the door...? A horrible object really, made of leather and horsehair, certainly not a thing of beauty. Flies were a continual problem in Egypt, to the extent that people didn't usually even bother to flick them away. It was quite normal to see babies with flies crawling over their faces. This handy device reproduces the action of a horse's tail and would easily kill six at a blow when whirled like one of those whirling dervishes we saw in action outside a mosque on one bizarre occasion. I gave it to my father as a jokey souvenir when we returned from our first tour. I cringe even now as I remember him sitting awkwardly with the thing waggling suggestively from his lap and my worldly-wise mother-in-law watching with wicked amusement. Since he died, the whisk came back to us and was hung by the study door. I might have got rid of it, but we lived near a pig farm and it could be just as fly-ridden as Egypt when they cleared out the sties.

It has to be said that I could probably dispose of most of these items (the pig farm has gone), and if I keep buying poetry books I may even have to. But I would fight to keep the camel bone and the papyrus certificate, along with something hanging between two sepia pen-and-ink sketches I made during the boat trip to Abu Simbel. It's a silver plate, edged with alternating lotus buds and flowers, with a finely etched image of the goddess Isis on it, taken from an original Nineteenth Dynasty portrait. Whoever made this had a sure hand. Isis is in profile, as usual, and wears a striking headdress – a vulture trailing its wings down behind her ear and across her braided hair, the neck and beak poking out as the cobra does from a pharaoh's head – and this is topped with what looks like a miniature temple, a pillared hypostyle hall. The eye of the goddess, etched into the plate's natural copper surface, is distinctively Egyptian, with its long, elegant backwards curve and its immaculate eyebrow. The nose is shapely, a nostril conjured with a single twist; the lips suggest a severity for all their fullness. This is the face of a determined deity, and the anonymous artist, sitting somewhere in a backstreet of Cairo, no doubt, has captured her so that she still speaks half a dynasty later. The detail of her jewelled necklace and her gown is beautifully handled, too. I still love this plate, though it cost only eight pounds from the Philae Bazaar. I have so many times used the story of Isis in my poetry and plays that it has meant a great deal to have the goddess nearby. The treachery of her brother-in-law, Seth, who killed Osiris and cut him into pieces which he scattered throughout the land, and Isis's long travels to gather up the pieces and fit them back together again, which she managed except that she couldn't find the penis... Apart from the fact that the story paralleled what was happening with the dissection and reconstruction of temples around Lake Nasser, it seemed to touch on what was troubling Jane's family, and the stage play I wrote in the 1980s and called *The Isis Myth* explores this. Although the name Isis is more readily associated with a terrorist movement these days, I hope that there is still some potency in the title. The play is a work I'm fond of. It has only ever been given a rehearsed reading at the Riverside Studios in Hammersmith when I think both the actors and the audience were rather baffled. It's rather too much (as Herodotus almost said) the gift of O'Neill.

There was just one occasion when we might have been tempted to load ourselves with worldly goods. We had been in the city of Sohag for a conference of volunteers, which turned out to be quite a lively occasion since, after much argument, we ended up voting to take a pay cut, idealistic souls that we were. The idealism, however, went hand in hand with materialism because one day we were taken to a suburb called Ahmim, originally Penopolis and the oldest continuously inhabited settlement in Egypt. The locals have nicknamed it 'Prehistoric Manchester' because of its fame as a producer of silk and cotton. Our friend Martin Spafford, one of the most mature and serious-minded of the volunteer clan, showed us around in company of a Muslim friend of his who lived there, and who evidently took great pride in his home. Ahmim is effectively built on a rubbish heap, a mound of Pharaonic, Greek and Roman debris and it is like one huge market, dominated by cotton and silk merchants. We first visited a rug-maker, who lived next door to Martin's friend, in a street rich with the stink of animals and crowded with the animals themselves – we had to pick our way past a water buffalo, donkeys and several vicious-looking camels to get into this house. There sat the master craftsman, for all the world like something out of medieval Europe. His loom was the most primitive of machines, his raw material torn-up strips salvaged from big factories, yet he produced from this unpromising material such exquisite rugs. The speed he worked at made it just possible to believe that he could turn out one a day: the prices he charged for them (LE2.50 each) seemed absurdly low, but we resisted. The Ahmim silk factory we visited was a further temptation. Natural silk, which was selling at something like £20 a metre back in the UK, was in Ahmim less than £3, although we held back again. We saw various stages of the weaving process at the back of the shop. No silkworms, though, since the thread is imported. I remember seeing towels being woven into incredibly intricate designs at top speed by an old man who used a simple hand-loom and who had worked there for forty years. There were larger machines on which those famous Egyptian cotton bedsheets are made. We bought a small towel for 40 piastres which still hangs on our heated rail for guests. And Jane – spurning local resources – sought out a woollen scarf, since the weather when we visited was decidedly chilly.

Once back in Aswan we would eventually have no scruples in loading up with cotton tablecloths from the market and the Philae Bazaar, some of which we still use regularly: once brightly decorated with ill-executed scenes from tomb paintings, now faded and tattered they are our most conspicuous link with our own ancient history. Those and the various woven baskets that we carried back, particularly one that for decades we used for dirty washing. This was the kind of basket that we would see in the souk filled with Aswan dates or peppers. It's the kind of basket that can be seen in pictures of Howard Carter's workers carrying sand away from Tutankhamun's tomb. It's the kind that features on paintings on tomb walls. And now it is in a black plastic bin liner in our shed, since the bottom eventually unravelled and could no longer be repaired.

If there's one thing I regret not having made room to bring back with us it's the *rababa*, the two-string fiddle that Jane bought for me for my birthday. Made from a decapitated coconut and a piece of animal- or fish-skin stretched across, I was able to use my fiddling skills to play anything anyone wanted. Sadly, no one really did want me to. Perhaps if it had been an *'oud*... In the end, it is not the artworks or souvenirs from the *souk* but the odd scraps of raw Egypt that attract me, playing their mysterious music of absence from the window ledges, and continually inviting me to make poems of them.

Samuel Baker

no history   no solid ground   each island
strong enough for a dinosaur to stand on
breaks away to form another colony   the *sudd*

spawns growth that has no destination   all
shapelessly rotting drift   a preyground
for crocodile and hippopotamus   for mosquitoes

and a hundred jotting flies   birds watch
then laugh us off   the islands shift like a game
of sliding each design into the vacant slot

no man has ever lived here   no woman
wanted children here   the empire of decay
it is an area as large as England

if you find the great lake   what then   what
will you do with it   they ask   the rain
sets in   call it Albert   demands for presents

more beads cups carpets   a better rifle
my fifty guinea gold chronometer
the months tick by   and we cannot move

they offer me a virgin in exchange for my wife
when we try to move   we sink   I watch
Florence fall into a purple clench of corruption

the sun beats us half mad   only the honey
memory   and the what might be   I dream
of the Source   of drinking at the Source

Loss

Discovery is inseparable from loss and among the many colourful characters associated with the Nile, two with whom we always felt a certain kinship were those 'Lovers on the Nile', the Bakers: the hunting, shooting son of a shipowner, Samuel and his second wife, blonde, Hungarian Florence. Not that we had anything in common with them except that they were a married couple on the upper reaches of a great river – yet Jane's personal history drew her repeatedly to stories of the African pioneers, Bruce, Burton, Speke, Stanley, and particularly Livingstone, because he began his travels in the house she lived in as a child on Zanzibar, with its louring shadows of the slave trade. These figures, so vividly described in Alan Moorhead's Nile books, were among the mighty handful to go in search of the river's Blue and White sources, but the Bakers managed to get lost in considerable style, for long periods stranded in the water-hyacinth nightmare of the *sudd*, an impenetrable swamp, and naturally carrying (or their servants carrying) the white man's burden: half the contents of a Victorian drawing room.

It would be good to think that gains and losses balance out in our lives, that there is some kind of cosmic *karma* at work. Nobody who lives abroad can escape the feeling that you are missing out on things at home, the birthdays and Christmases, the little local happenings, shifts in the domestic zeitgeist and the events that never quite make it across the Channel. But living on the banks of the Nile makes one philosophical about such matters and – even without the annual inundation – breeds a Heraclitian view of the world, ever flowing, ever changing. Leaving behind parents and elderly grandparents, there's always the fear that they may not be there when you return. I know how traumatic my elder daughter found it when my mother died while she was on a similar venture to ours, not in Egypt but in a remote corner of Hunan Province, China. At least we had phones and email, but it was a difficult experience. In our case, the worry was Jane's mother, who had had a severe stroke before we left. She lost the power of speech for a while, though it eventually returned and we probably would not have left if it had not seemed that she was getting better, off the drink, more lucid, apparently on the mend. We made the decision to come, but we knew that there was a risk. In our second year, we probably compounded the anxiety by agreeing to let my sister-in-law Amanda come back with us to Aswan. It would help her escape the gloom of her home circumstances and let her sample the exotic pleasures beyond Teddington Lock, Bushy Park and Hampton Court Maze. Her mother must have missed her and I see things more from a parent's point of view now I am of a similar age, but I still think it was the right thing to do and having the company of Tode (as we still call her) was a great pleasure. It was the beginning of a global lifestyle for her (India, Yemen, Ethiopia, Georgia) in the company of Tim, the American she would spend her life with – once she had fought off the attentions of certain over-enthusiastic young Egyptian suitors.

There was an abiding and paradoxical sense of impermanence during our two years as we looked across the Nile at a view that has barely changed in millennia. It was partly that we were slowly becoming aware of just how precarious VSO's role in Egypt was, but we could also not escape the fact that we were, like Matthew Arnold, 'wandering between two worlds, one dead,/The other powerless to be born'. We had left nothing of consequence and had nothing of consequence to go back to. We basked on the shore of circumstance like Nile monitors enjoying the moment. Something of this melancholy expressed itself in the more bleak and oblique poems I wrote, including one that has had various titles from 'An Ageing Couple in Aswan' to 'Last Day' to the mischievous 'Welcome at Aswan'. I was not saying anything here about our own marriage, which was 'degged with dew, dappled with dew', but rather imagining a weary pair of Western tourists ending their holiday (as many do) and perhaps their relationship as they reached the First Cataract:

We have seen the sights.
What's left?

the mausoleum in my head
the broken obelisk in our bed
the reconstruction of all I've said
on your separate island

and ahead

the yellow drifts of the dead
the days bereft
and the long rock nights

Looking back, what I was losing without really noticing it was my loyalty to the conventional church, which had been very important to me only a year or two before. At the same time, there was a spiritual cornucopia before me, which swirled Islamic and Coptic ingredients even while it brimmed a rich Yeatsian magic. I have never subscribed to the view that humankind grows wiser as the ages pass. The Ancient Egyptians clearly knew a great deal about many things that mean nothing to us. Imagine someone in five thousand years' time finding the remains of a computer manual or the last surviving set-top digital TV box. Wouldn't the Wallis Budge and John Romer and Zahi Hawass of that age expound wonderful theories as to the cults and beliefs surrounding these things? Would they have any idea of the kind of magic that they were capable of: online shopping at the great god *Tesco* or images of the mighty leader of the tribe X, *Si-mon-cow-ell*? I suspect that there are powers within the temples to which we have simply lost the key. I suspect too that many of the texts take for granted mental and psychic abilities which we have neglected so entirely that they barely operate today, or if they do we are unable to acknowledge their potency, dismissing them as coincidence or ignoring them. Champollion's tenacious work on the Rosetta Stone gave us the language of the hieroglyphs, but what it could not give us is a way to access the magic. Partly this is because we do not know what the language of the ancients actually sounded like and the uttering aloud of texts has always been a vital part of magic rituals. Like Ted Hughes, who created an experimental language, Orghast, with these ideas in mind, I am a firm believer in the power of the music of the spoken word to make things happen. I say this not only as one who has encouraged halls full of children to shout *abracadabra*, but one who has felt the force of the voiced utterance, the potency of prayer. But until someone discovers a way of recreating the sounds of the past through replaying prints in clay made on a spinning potter's wheel as one might lower a stylus into a spinning groove (a theory propounded in all seriousness), then we can only guess at what *The Book of the Dead* sounded like. To be honest, most people would not be very interested even if we could recreate the sounds. We are much more intrigued by reconstructions of feats of engineering or examining the processes of mummification than in wondering whether there might actually be something in the theory of the *ba* and the *ka*, the elements of the human being that were believed to live on after death. We are also culturally conditioned to be sceptical of, wary of magic, though religion is magic in respectable clothing, and while I don't know about Mohammed, certainly Jesus was not averse to the odd magical show stopper.

By living in Egypt, by spending so much time in the presence of the ancient world, I was quietly laying the foundations for the Jungian I would become, never abandoning Christianity, but no longer in thrall to its more bourgeosified and stultifying structures. I am sure that in many ways the religion of Ancient Egypt was shocking and barbaric, and I can readily imagine that Akhenaten's reaction to the behaviour of the Priests at Thebes was because of what he saw as corruption and human folly in the 'church'. What intrigues me is how much it all mattered to these people and that they never lost their belief in the power of what we would call today the supernatural. Moreover, they took the fact of a life beyond the body quite for granted, whereas in contemporary Christianity it is something that is apologised for and regarded as at best an embarrassment to intelligent modern minds. At the same time, the lengths to which the ancients went to ensure that their bodies were preserved after death tells us how much they did not want to lose what they had on this side of the tomb. The sensuality of their art shows how dearly in love they were with physical existence. But they had a knowledge that we have lost. Not a Da Vinci Code secret, but something that has disappeared into the corners of the New Age fringe, into yoga classes and psychic fairs, into publications from The Society for Psychical Research and dubious documentaries on exotic digital channels.

But modern Egypt has lost this too. In many ways, the values of the Ancients are more amenable to Westerners than to the present-day Egyptians, whose history is a palimpsest. The original culture of tomb and temple has been repeatedly overlain by foreign influences, obscured by non-Egyptian values and for the past few hundreds of years (though it remains avowedly secular) Islamic ideals. Pharaonic worship was centred on images of the human form – its colossi, its wall-paintings, even its alphabet – but it is considered shameful in Islam to draw any representation of Allah's creation. Thus, the only imagery to be found in mosques is of mosaic designs and ornate calligraphy (profound traditions of music, voice and dance, of philosophy and debate, compensate to some extent) and the visual arts are neither taught nor encouraged. It is not surprising then that many of the Egyptians we met seemed indifferent to their heritage, showed few regrets for what had been lost or found and showed little sense of connection with the world of the pharaohs, though ever willing to try and make a living from it. What does worry them is the loss of prestige and influence in the contemporary world. Not so long ago Egypt was in a strong position to negotiate a permanent seat on the Security Council of the UN. But now, as Tarek Osman says in *Egypt on the Brink*, while Brazil, South Africa, Turkey, Saudi Arabia are regularly asked to attend G20 summits, 'Egypt is hardly ever invited'. The still unravelling consequences of the 2011 uprising may yet change all that: an undeniable pride of ownership did begin to emerge in some of the cities. But it was always going to be difficult to pull back from so many decades of decline since the heyday of Nasser, when the nation could stand up to the Western Powers and be respected.

Not everything that is lost is to be regretted. I found myself some months ago talking to an English couple who had known Alexandria before the days of the last revolution, when King Farouk ('King of Egypt and Sudan, Sovereign of Nubia, of Kordofan, and of Darfur') was in power. My host had even been patted on the head by him. They were reminiscing, sad at what had been lost but at the same time remarking on what an unpleasant individual he was – including the fact that, along with his other little indulgences (six hundred oysters a week, wild shopping sprees) he would appear in public with a tame leopard. It's not a leopard that rises before my eyes now as the adequate symbol for this portion of my book, but a dung beetle of the kind we often spotted when we were walking in the desert. The sacred scarab – the god Khepri – pushes a world of dung before it, the droppings and debris of others rolled up into his personal universe, much as a poet gathers and garners whatever scraps he or she can find and keeps on going.

The Scarab Cake

Our daughter's chosen birthday cake's
a scarab: she's been studying
Egyptians. Here, among my books
the lapis lazuli is hidden,
its icing hard and blue, its sun
a chocolate orange rolling on
into her teens. This scarab seal
was Khepri or 'He Who Becomes',
whose little dung ball used to roll
down obelisks, papyri, tombs,
but finished up with souvenirs
that Westerners hang from their ears
at birthday parties. Rosie's ten,
and that seems like a dynasty
to her. But think back twenty, when
we lived in Egypt – then, how we
ruled our Old Kingdom! All that waste
collected, shaped, and dribbled west
on camel spoors, until we found
this campsite. Scarabs symbolise
the dawn of hope of dawn, how ground
can breed new stars, and tantalise
us into thinking it's not wrong
to spend a lifetime pushing dung.
The roller-skating party's over:
at last, the scarab cake appears,
its candles lit, its sun-disc shivered
to moon pieces. How many years
have we done this? Sing. Take the knife.
And share the sweets of future life.

CALLS TO PRAY AND PLAY

The call to prayer sounds five times a day from loudspeakers on the minarets of Egyptian mosques. It is an acquired taste. Before the 2011 revolution, residents of Cairo had been growing increasingly irritated by the cacophony of unsynchronised and overlapping calls across the city and the process of computerising, centralising and so homogenising the broadcasts from over 4,500 mosques had begun. What stage this has reached, I do not know, but life in Cairo will certainly be less vibrant without that wash of sound, surreal as it was. In Aswan in the early 'eighties, there were far fewer mosques, but if you were unlucky enough to have a flat next door to one, you might find yourself woken abruptly by the crackle and acoustic feedback that accompanied every *Allahu Akbar*. The prayer begins with these words sung out four times and however others might react to being woken or disturbed by them, I could never resist the beauty of the sound. Hearing it today instantly brings back our life in Egypt. *Muezzin* – the men, always men, who sang the prayer – were traditionally blind, apparently so that they could not use the high tower (the minaret) in order to spy on private lives. For centuries, of course, there would have been no amplification, which must have considerably enhanced the effect and been glorious to hear. Muslims are fortunate that the Arabic of *Allahu Akbar* is so mellifluous to the ear: 'God is Great' is such a clipped, unresonant phrase by comparison, and the contemporary usage of 'great' doesn't help: '*Eastenders* is great... Wayne Rooney is great'. The prayer continues (though transcriptions vary): *Ashhadu anna la ilaha illa Allah* – I bear witness that there is no god but the One God, which is then repeated. This is followed by *Ashhadu anna Muhammadan Rasul Allah* – I bear witness that Mohammed is the messenger of God (repeated) and the very distinctive rising music of *Hayya 'ala-s-Salah, Hayya 'ala-l-Falah* (Hurry to/rise up for the prayer, to success/salvation) and a final repetition of *Allahu Akbar* and signing off on the wonderfully labial *La ilaha illa Allah*, There is no god but the One God. Apparently, the pre-dawn prayer also inserts a line about prayer being better than sleep: *As-salatu Khayrun Minan-nawm*.

Although these sounds have pleasant associations for me, Islam in Egypt has been turbulent since we left and there have been a number of uprisings and outrages. The most widely reported before the revolution was the massacre of fifty-eight tourists at the temple of Deir el Bahri in 1997. But we should not forget that the 9/11 terrorists had strong Egyptian connections: one of the pilots involved was the son of a Cairo lawyer, and Bin Laden's right-hand man was Ayman al-Zawahari, leader of 'Islamic Jihad' who were behind the assassination of Sadat. The Muslim Brotherhood had electoral success in the early years of this century, becoming ever more sophisticated and less repellently radical, but there was a mass purge in 2008 when over eight hundred members were arrested and twenty-five ended up in jail. Such severe crackdowns left a legacy of resentment which was one of the causes of the Arab Spring. The Brotherhood, astonishingly enough, would go on to win half the seats in the 2011-12 elections, and it was their man, Mohammed Morsi, who took the Presidency before the next upheaval.

The novelist Aal al Aswany captures the background to all this within the largely satirical context of *The Yacoubian Building*, which appeared in Arabic in 2002. We knew many keen young working-class students like Aswany's Taha, who is the son of a 'mere' doorkeeper like our own Shukri. He achieves brilliant exam results at school and his one ambition is to join the police force. Aswany describes the job interview, where everything seems to be going well until just as he is leaving the room the 'presiding general' casually asks what his father's profession is. From that moment it is clear that Taha will never become a policeman and he is inexorably drawn into the extreme Islamicist activities at his university. Aswany portrays the ruthless character of Sheikh Muhammad Shakir in a manner that is revealing for Western readers – how he stresses in his Friday sermons the need to see everything from an Islamic point of view, to have feelings towards other people only in relation to how well they observe Allah's Law and the paramount need for *jihad* (one of those foreign words that has established itself in English, as *perestroika* did). In Aswany's novel, Taha's Islamicist aspirations are diverted and confused after he is taken by the police and vilely tortured. From then on, he is driven by a need for brutal revenge rather than anything nobly spiritual.

I was not much less naive than Taha during our years in Upper Egypt and just as impressionable. While not exactly a fundamentalist, resisting the Billy Graham urgings of the Christian Union, I had been a fairly active Methodist at university. By the time we went to Aswan, I still had a strong religious instinct as I do today, though now it resembles those temples we visited buried by decades of sand and rubbish. Jane and I had even applied to teach with a missionary organisation before approaching VSO, going through the initial vetting procedure during which it became apparent that it really wasn't for us. I don't know what we were thinking, or how we imagined we could cope. I remember making cynical little narratives out of the inkblots they gave us on the Rorschach test, which didn't go down well with the rather po-faced board. It wasn't quite as bad as Taha's interview, but it was one of the most embarrassing I've ever had. To the organisation's credit, they did gently suggest that we might try a secular route – maybe Voluntary Service Overseas?

It has always been through my senses that any spiritual call reaches me and especially through music, the most potent force in my life. I know what Walter Pater meant when he said that all art aspires to the condition of music. As far as I am concerned, he might well have replaced 'art' with 'all life'. Pythagoras understood something vital when he suggested the existence of the music of the spheres and those regimes that have tried to control music knew exactly what they had to deal with. Shostakovich, meanwhile, has conquered the world, and the Soviet Union has disintegrated. There were a few musical summonses during our Egyptian tour, one of the strangest being when I heard a man on a simple squeeze-box in the school playground picking out a familiar tune. It was an Arab folk song, evidently, but it was familiar because Rimsky Korsakov uses it in *Sheherazade*. Street musicians would occasionally catch the ear, too, even a snake charmer once. But it was the unearthly, everyday music of the *muezzin* that affected me most. When I came to write a one-man play about Gordon of Khartoum in 1984 (almost a hundred years after his death) I knew I wanted to use that sound as part of the action. I selected extracts from David Fanshawe's remarkable *African Sanctus*, a choral work which incorporates the composer's own field recordings of local music into his setting of the mass – the effect is similar to the well-known track by the Hilliard Ensemble and the saxophonist Jan Garbarek: soulful moaning on a soft bed of choral harmony. I wrote the play – based closely on Gordon's own journals and our old favourite Alan Moorhead's *The White Nile* – for an actor friend of mine, Stephen Hanvey, and we took it to the Edinburgh Fringe. I was in charge of the sound and the moment towards the end when the *muezzin* starts up I always found very moving in Steve's performance. Considering that we were competing with a production of *The Lion, the Witch and the Wardrobe* upstairs, we didn't do so badly, though there was that occasion when only one person turned up and having negotiated with the audience, we all went to the pub.

The Gordon play is not about Egypt, although it was up the Nile that the great man was looking for help and through areas familiar to us that Kitchener would come to settle the score, firstly as part of the 'heavy lumbering column' that arrived too late to save Gordon and later (via Kitchener's Island, Aswan) as commander and hero of Omdurman. It would have been impossible for me to write without the experience of living so far into Africa and knowing what it felt like to be cut off (and fighting a losing battle in the case of my teaching). I could empathise with the notion of someone called to a particular task, too, which – on reflection – could be what made us think that we could work as missionaries. In my play, which I eventually called *Between the Two Niles*, Gordon is presented as himself a religious fundamentalist and his bête noire, the Mahdi (somewhat prefiguring the extremists of Islamic State) is seen as the Hyde to his Jekyll. This is how it ends:

GORDON: The British must come. They will come today or the next day.

(*At his telescope*).

Give me fifty men only...

The White Nile has filled the ditch, levelled the rampart and rendered the land-mines innocuous. Now there is a fifteen hundred yard stretch of gleaming mud...

(*Scribbles a note*)

'We want you to come quickly.'

(*Explosion nearby*)

I died long ago. It did not produce a twitter in me.

(*Silence*).

He is not ashamed of his God.

Find me the man and I will take him as my help, who utterly despises money, name, glory, honours, one who never wishes to see his home again, one who looks to God as the source of good, controller of evil...

(*Pause*)

When I returned to Southampton from Shanghai, I didn't want to be picked out from the crowd as the conquering hero, so I had them tie my new suit in a bundle and tow it behind us in the sea...

(*Stands, defiant*)

Go tell the Mahdi that I have only to stamp on the ground and you shall be surrounded by the Army of Her Majesty the Queen before whom you will not be able to stand!

(*Sinks into chair, then up again, towards window. As if speaking to citizens:*)

Tomorrow, the steamers cannot fail to arrive. I myself will not go aboard, lest I be outranked by the newcomers and ordered to leave Khartoum, but all senior officers should put on full dress uniform to give a real welcome...

And meanwhile, everyone who can carry arms from eight to eighty must man the defences...

(*Pause. Then shouts:*)

Play!

(*Ill-disciplined military band plays*)

The English... will be here... in 24 hours.

(*He returns to room*)
The people will no longer believe me. I have told them over and over again that help will come, but it has never come and now they must see I tell them lies.

The game is up – and Rule Britannia.

(*Music dissipates*)

Go and collect all the people you can on the lines and make a good stand. Now leave me to smoke these cigarettes. I want oysters when I come home — with brown bread — lots of them, not just a dozen, but four dozen.
(*Silence*)

I wish I were the Mahdi.

(*Light fades leaving him in silhouette. Now he speaks as the Mahdi, giving replies to his own questions*)

MAHDI: Whomsoever you encounter in battle — saving only Gordon Pasha, may God protect him from every evil — whomsoever you encounter, kill him. God has said, 'Their belief in Me only after they have seen my might profiteth them nothing'. (*Shouting:*) Do you intend to attack Khartoum tomorrow morning?

GORDON: Yes, Lord of All.

MAHDI: Will you advance with pure hearts and full determination to fight in God's cause?

GORDON: Yes!

MAHDI: Even if two thirds of you should perish!

GORDON: Yes!

(*He removes his shoes and faces the audience. He holds his hands to the lobes of his ears, then lowers them, left within right, and kneels in the Muslim act of prayer*)

In the name of Allah, the merciful, the compassionate. Praise be to Allah, the Lord of the worlds, the merciful and compassionate, the Prince of the day of judgment, Thee we serve and to Thee we pray for help; lead us in the right way, the way of those to whom thou hast shown mercy...

(*In the customary manner, the prayer is concluded by looking over his right and then his left shoulders. Ostensibly this is to acknowledge the two recording angels. Here, there is also a nervousness of looking behind to see who is approaching.*

Blackout.

Kyrie from David Fanshawe's African Sanctus.)

I was always interested by D.H.Lawrence's rhetorical question (was it to himself? or in a letter?) – why does the artist have to be so religious? I can't find the original context, but I imagine it was an exasperated cry about his own condition passed off as an observation on artists in general. Yet there is a truth which I recognise. The artist is after all playing God, at being a creator. But I believe too that someone writing creatively, particularly writing with the intensity that poetry demands, is taking soundings of the same areas of the psyche as someone praying. As with prayer, those soundings might not go very far, but they are potentially bottomless. I suspect that this is a truth familiar to that very fine poet, the former Archbishop of Canterbury, Rowan Williams (well known, incidentally, to our Aswani colleague, Stuart Evans, who was called – literally by a voice, he told us – to join the Church of Wales when he returned home). Poetry is about truth, the search for the most truthful way of expressing something, or finding an experience's 'true name' as Ursula Le Guin's Wizard of Earthsea might have put it.

Unlike Stuart, my vocation was not to be missionary or minister, but poet. Those were the deep waters that attracted me, crocodile infested, bilharzia-laden or not. So in I plunged. And doing so I feel very close to the priest – at least as close as I do to the role of teacher, which is the role most people have seen me in, the one that will pay for my pension. I have been a teacher by default, because I could not think of any other way to earn a living while I wrote, but it's not an incompatible profession and there is room (as Lawrence showed) for the didactic muse, even for a poem about teaching as heartfelt as his 'Last Lesson of the Afternoon', which concludes 'I shall sit and wait for the bell'. I have never forgotten a visit we made to the Regents Park mosque during our VSO induction course, when we were addressed by a local Imam, who told us that Mohammed had said that a teacher was almost a prophet. I don't know what Mohammed thought of poets – more than Plato did, I trust. But if Egypt offered me employment as a teacher, it was calling me as a writer, and it had been calling me for years without my realising it.

When I drew a Moses basket on the Nile in my primary

school notebook or made a *shaduf* out of a pencil and plasticine; when I ordered my plastic after-dinner joke in which King Tut mysteriously would not stay in his magnetic coffin; when I had to choose a poem to learn off by heart and my mother suggested 'Ozymandias', it was calling. When I had to take my penfriend to London for the day and my father recommended Sir John Soanes Museum and Sety I's sarcophagus; when my grandfather jokingly said 'Egg-white' every time he found an Egypt stamp for my sister's album; when I learnt about the Aswan dam in O-Level Geography or queued to see the Tutankhamun Exhibition at the British Museum or read Thor Heyerdal's *Ra* or studied *All for Love* and *Antony and Cleopatra* at A-Level, it was calling, Egypt, calling. And when I wrote my first proper poem, in 1974, it kept on calling through the dodgy metre, the hackneyed diction ('All their lives the Egyptians built pyramids/To entomb their Pharaohs in beauty,/To enfold their treasures in linen and stone,/Layer on layer, to embalm their beauty...') and in spite of the facile juxtaposition in which 'slaves ...would see/A bright butterfly living for the day...'. But it wasn't just Egypt calling me, it was the voice of poetry itself.

The Empty Quarter

Lionhead, foxpelt, oryx horns,
my old service rifles in their rack,
these tablets, this scotch, and a map

of the Rub el Khali ('What is he
talking about? What does he want?):
the Sands, the Empty Quarter...

Is it enough to remain an Englishman,
no longer The Christian? Or enough
to slouch, replete, and alone,

after a pork lunch, windows
Chubb-bolted against intruders,
their watch-towers, telephones?

Bismillah el Rahman el Rahim...
Something calls from beyond this flap –
a wolf? The one that killed

two children at their water-hole?
Or my dawn summons – the profane
brass bell of a coffee mortar?

Like a lighthouse I tower here, but –
El Nasrani! El Nasrani! – am conspicuously
inferior. These are Muslim, these are Bedu,

'The English' is an unknown tribe,
or known as the infidel. My excuses
parch: their Sands drink, drink.

Brick wastes of England. Dunes
that have gutters and aerials. Horizon
strapped to the wrist, our distances

are dates and coloured tubes,
Alum Bay egg-timers,
budgerigar and hamster cages...

'Guide us on the straight path',
our minds are sand, stuffed
against the sun, against moon-raids,

not equipped for the shifting, sinking
one path, which is only camel dung
(could be camel dung, could be raiders....)

I am alert. ('Better cold and wet
than to wake with a dagger in your ribs').
But what am I hunting? An extinct,

not mythological creature – and one
that could survive without this shell,
but only in deserts at the mind's end.

The Libyan, the Arabian, and Other Deserts

When I read Wilfred Thesiger's account of 'the Empty Quarter' in his classic travel book, *Arabian Sands*, Egypt returned to me forcefully. This was 1983, and the poem I wrote shortly afterwards is an oblique expression of love for a lost world, drawing on some of our own experiences of encounters with bedouin and life in the desert but also recreating that feeling of being an outsider, of having your preconceptions challenged. The poem (first published, aptly, in *Encounter*) is a lament too for a certain kind of dry, barren English existence – the suburban deserts I had grown up with and that both Jane and I were determined not to return to. And reading it now it's clear that much of the poem's emotion comes from the circumstances we found ourselves in when we arrived home. Even though we had spent a year and a half adjusting to the radically altered landscape of our lives, by the time I wrote 'The Empty Quarter' we still had not left our new 'Waste Land', and I fear we are even now on its fringes. After the Alexandria ceremony, we had flown straight home. I was clutching my 'gold' medal and we were full of the experiences of another year in Egypt, keen to talk about it and look at the photos my parents had developed for us. We had agreed to go from Heathrow to their house in Eastcote first, where we were welcomed and feted. There was wine and food and shared stories and news – we might have entered a scene from one of the Tombs of the Nobles. But it was a fateful decision, because that night Jane's mother – before she had even seen her daughter again – took her own life.

'The Empty Quarter' brings to the surface feelings that had been buried since 1981 when we woke up to find ourselves in a wilderness that was very different from any Thesiger knew. The stars went on shining, the beasts went on feeding, but we were in a new place and we had to survive. Our temporary camp was Arbroath where we found ourselves working with a different kind of nomad: the Boat People who had made the perilous journey from Vietnam to Hong Kong. Ethnic Chinese mainly, these poor people had been granted asylum in Britain and we were teaching them to speak English, helping them adapt to our exotic lifestyle. To most of these Vietnamese, Northeast Scotland itself felt like a desert, because to them there never seemed to be anyone on the streets. Vietnam is densely populated, Hong Kong even more so. Most of the refugees we taught found the thin population of Scotland terrifying and they eventually left and ended up in the English city ghettoes that the authorities had been trying to keep them out of in the first place. In all this, Egypt was pushed into the wings. 'The Empty Quarter' is the first creative evidence that it was trying to assert itself again, although it wasn't my first return to the desert. One of the best things I wrote in Arbroath was a sequence of thirty-six sonnets about the Winter Journey that some of Captain Scott's men made in 1911 to look for specimens of the Emperor Penguin's egg. Wildernesses cold or hot were evidently at the back of my mind. Perhaps they are at the back of the mind of all young poets after T.S.Eliot? They only ceased to have any appeal to this poet once we had children.

Childless as we were, living indeed where there was no fertile strip, desert was something we took for granted in Aswan. I cycled every morning between the red rocks of the Eastern Desert and the dunes on the far side of the Nile where the Libyan Desert begins, but was generally more concerned with dodging animals or negotiating carts of watermelon. As I have mentioned, Egyptians are traditionally very wary of the desert, an abominable place of demons and unimaginable dangers, the 'Red Land' as opposed to the life-giving 'Black Land' in ancient lore. But we did find exceptions such as a friend of Alan's, another Ahmed, who took us to see his village. Khubbaneya is on a peninsula some distance north of Aswan, where the Nile is about half a mile wide and there are the beginnings of a fertile strip (sprouting maize, plots of clover, young banana plantations) although the desert still comes very close to the water. Apparently, the village used to be cut off altogether during the months of inundation, but since the High Dam, it has been permanently connected with the desert on the West Bank. What impressed me as Ahmed took us through his village was the way he spoke in almost romantic tones of the beauties of the surrounding countryside, launching into a passionate hymn of praise to the desert, the excursions he and his friends had made out there, the nearby mountain peaks they had climbed, how they'd go out and camp in the wilderness for days on end just for the fun of it, to relish the sunsets and the views. They went well armed, he assured us, because of the snakes (the *tresha*, sidewinders that are capable of leaping and biting a man on a camel – we've seen their tyre-track marks in the sand) and the jackals. It was refreshing to meet an Egyptian who seemed to understand and even share the British obsession with deserts.

The British do have that reputation. Even before Lawrence of Arabia, who established the archetype with some help from David Lean, Peter O'Toole, and a ravishing soundtrack, there had been the fittingly-named Doughty, for example, whose *Travels in Arabia Deserta* became the Bible for later travellers such as Freya Stark and Thesiger himself. Then there is the Second World War, in which the key engagement was a desert battle. As a poet, the name that immediately occurs to me is that of Keith Douglas who was a tank commander at El Alamein. There is an ironic spin on the word in Douglas's case, however as he 'deserted' from his HQ in 1942, but not to escape battle, to seek it out. His prose memoir *Alamein to Zem Zem*, one of the best pieces of literature to emerge from that period, tells the story. He spent time in Alexandria and Cairo too, both of which feature in his poems, but the desert is in them everywhere. We found after our return to England that every other man of a certain age that we met seemed to have been in Egypt during the Second World War. Jane's own grandfather had been there during the First War, too, and remembered camel stew: the meat was tough, he told us, but you got 'a nice drop of gravy'.

Our own treks into the desert were memorable and often overwhelmingly exhausting, but driving through the desert had its moments too. We had crossed its periphery on hair-raising taxi rides to and from temples, and there was the occasional brief foray, usually when we went out towards the High Dam, where a new university (the University of Africa) was being established in desert terrain, or if we had to go to the airport. In those days it was not an international airport and all very low key. You stepped straight from the plane on to the tarmac, probably very glad to feel the baking ground beneath your feet (when one friend flew in with EgyptAir they had to turn back because they were missing a wheel). It was a bold enterprise for my parents to travel out to see us and it meant a lot to me. On the morning of their very early arrival we found there was no water in our flat so we had had to dash early over to the home of my future brother-in-law, Tim, who worked for CARE. Tim had generously offered to drive us to the airport. It was a stunning morning, sun rising and moon setting over the desert as we drove, and the light of the Airbus approaching along the valley of the Nile. I can see it now, their figures stepping down from the single plane on the tarmac, nothing but desert on all sides. It had a mythical quality, Spielbergish, but also curiously what I imagine it might be like to arrive in the afterlife. Charles Causley (whom I had met in Exeter only a couple of years before this) captures the dream-like feeling in his poem 'Eden Rock', which imagines his parents beckoning from the far side of a 'drifted stream' and calling to him 'Crossing is not as hard as you might think'.

Flying over it in moonlight or crossing it on a camel may well be the best way to experience desert. Going through it by bus is definitely not, but that was the method we chose to travel the hundred miles from the Nile to the Red Sea. Failing the romanticised overview that EgyptAir could provide, I suspect that a narrowing of focus is what you need to fully appreciate such landscapes so that you learn to distinguish between, for instance, different kinds of camel dung (there are as many words among the Bedouin as Eskimos have for snow) or the precise location of a forgotten Roman well. No doubt if you have an eye for exploitation, your focus will be on schist, talc, dolerite, porphyry, quartz, emerald, sapphire and gold (not forgetting oil), all of which are found northeast of Aswan. What is not found is the most precious of all: water. The Arabian or Eastern Desert is considered less hospitable than the Libyan Desert, simply because there aren't the oases. What I remember of that bus journey from Qena to Safaga is the surprising variety of the scenery, not only monotonous stretches of sand (though there are those) but ruggedly dramatic mountainous terrain. The Ancient Egyptians called the region 'Land of the Akhitiu' and for them it was a useful barrier between the Nile and potential invaders. There have always been trade routes across it, bringing supplies in the earliest days from Arabia, Somalia and India, and frequently used for transporting slaves. The Romans characteristically extended the number of available roads, but many of these crossings exist only as camel tracks. The tarmacked route we took from Qena had also been one of the favourite ways for Muslims to reach Mecca (the Christians preferred to become hermits) but since the opening of the Suez Canal and the invention of the jumbo jet, people don't cross the desert unless they have to or unless they are eccentric British travellers. Guidebooks speak of that vague murmuring sound, the grating of a billion billion sand grains, but sadly there is no chance of hearing this from an Egyptian gas-guzzler, any more than you are going to be able to sample the famously pure, enigmatically scented air or see a scarab beetle scuttle away from your shoes. This wasn't *The Desert Song*, in other words, but the reality of grubby necessity: getting from A to B where there's nothing in-between. That 'nothing', however, does reach 6,000 feet at times and to my somewhat homesick gaze even resembled the kind of scenery you might see around a Scottish loch. Perhaps because of the time of year we travelled (April), there was almost always some trace of green.

As I have suggested, the deserts that make up most of Egypt have offered rich pickings for industry, but much of the art has its origins there too. I'm sorry that we never managed to get to the alabaster quarries which weren't so very far from Aswan – alabaster was a regular feature of the tourist shops. And what about all those garnets and lapis that you could buy for so little in the Philae Bazaar? They were out there somewhere. As were the azurite and frit, the malachite used for blue and green. We had walked on the iron oxide whenever we climbed the hill behind our flat. There lay the skin tones for all those figures in the Tombs of the Nobles.

If the Eastern Desert is a gateway to the rest of the world, the Western has been a source of mirages. The biggest of these for many years was the Qattar Depression project, a wild scheme to divert water from the Mediterranean into the huge depression south of El Alamein. When we were in Egypt this was often mentioned and mocked as a castle in the air, something that would happen *bukra fil mish-mish* – tomorrow when the apricots bloom, i.e. never. Yet as the population has been doubling and dependence on foreign food has been increasing (Egypt is the world's largest wheat importer), engineers have been at work on something equally impressive: a scheme to reclaim over half a million acres of desert, beginning at that broadest part of Lake Nasser where we had our brush with disaster. The year before we came to Aswan, in fact, the work had begun on a new water course (predictably called the Sadat Canal) which would feed water from Wadi Toshka out into the Western Desert and eventually link up with the Kharga Oasis or even the far-flung Dakhla Oasis. This was part of the New Valley scheme, whereby a second Nile valley would be created, taking 10% of the river's water, and expanding the available living area in the country by anything up to a quarter. The new canal would follow an ancient dried-up tributary valley of the Nile along a line of residual oases. By the 1990s the project was already irrigating a large area northwest of the lake and in 2005 the – inevitably – Mubarak Pumping Station was opened near Lake Nasser. It is spoken of as one of the most impressive engineering achievements in

Egypt since the High Dam itself, not least because the area where it was constructed is seismically active and endures temperatures from freezing point to 50 degrees. There have been critics and it remains to be seen what will become of the project, due to have been finished by 2020, now that power has shifted away from Mubarak's cronies.

Mubarak was still a mere vice-president as we set off on our journey across the desert to Alexandria. Imagining what Alexander the Great's own approach must have been like, I produced a poem (see p. 157) which has never been published but is very much in the mould of those in *Westerners*. I called it 'Next' because I read somewhere that Howard Carter announced as he removed the last of the objects from Tutankhamun's tomb that his next project would be to search for the lost tomb of Alexander the Great. He obviously didn't notice time's winged chariot behind him. By 1939, all he had to look forward to were 'deserts of vast eternity'.

Quarry

A fitting monument
to lost potency
this broken pencil,

this obelisk that was
never raised, but lay
unithyphallically

in the deep deep south
of Upper Egypt
and remains unmoved

by the provocation of lens
and legs astride it.
Stone slot, I wish

to leave Silicon Valley,
no longer to wait
on Michelangelo

or that other virus.
Admit me through the screen
of my beaded years

to your warm presence.
Tell them on the Thames
Embankment and in Place

de la Concorde, tell them
at the National Trust
in Kingston Lacey,

and in the deserts
of Washington, to begin
the countdown

without me. Mouth
of stone. Let the day's
damp wedges

swell until you
split the sun-seeker free.
Let it be called SOHO.

Let it scent Apollo.

SOME OASES

What prompted the poem 'Quarry' in 1991, apart from the unsettling New Jersey heat and a sense of time running out, was seeing the Washington Monument, which – unlike the over-ambitious cracked one lying in Aswan – would indeed become the world's tallest obelisk. An oasis is not always a source of water in a desert. It might be as dry and desolate a spot as that granite quarry, which I loved and which I was revisiting in imagination at my desk in Leigh Street, Clinton. In my poem the unraised rock becomes a physical manifestation of that block every writer struggles to move, but its persistence tells me just how much Egypt endured in my mind. I was still being drawn back there ten years on, looking for whatever it was that had mattered so much to me, something timeless in every sense, something that aims only for enlightenment. I was a real teacher now, and father of a five-year-old but whatever I did, wherever we travelled, that pink granite truth would remain in Aswan, and I would remain true to it. Our year in America was in itself a kind of oasis, but a very small one in our lives by comparison with Egypt, a mere water-hole.

In fact, the Faiyum was the only literal oasis we visited while we were there and even that is sometimes called 'an oasis which is not an oasis' because it is linked by a corridor of green to the Nile. It is the biggest and least remote, a relatively short ride out west from Beni Suef, which is itself well on the way to Cairo. We went there ostensibly for one of the VSO conferences, which tended to be talking shops, opportunities for venting spleen and for making ill-judged decisions: at the previous meeting in Sohag we had voted ourselves a pay-cut. There was a growing sense of futility about the entire VSO Egypt programme by this time and it was wound up shortly after we completed our two years. Indeed, VSO itself changed its character as they encouraged more and more professionals of retirement age to participate, and the final couple who went to Aswan after us were about the age we are now. These conferences were, I suppose, a chance to ponder the broader issues, but such pondering could raise more questions than it answered. It would have been more helpful if we had been offered a refresher course in Arabic, since everything came down to knowing the language. We had sat through a pre-tour language course, but all I retain of that is how one volunteer could never grasp that 'yes' was *aiwa* and kept saying *awi* and we giggled so much that poor Ali our teacher sent someone out. Arabic is no laughing matter, even in its colloquial form although a lot of it has stuck and even now Jane and I chatter away in phrase-book style: *Ows shai?* (want tea?), *Fain?* (Where are you? – useful as a text message). And much to the confusion of our guests, when we say 'Where's the otter?' we are simply falling back on Arabic for cat: *'otta*.

Some things did get changed as a result of these get-togethers. It was decided while we were in the Faiyum that instead of my being based permanently in one school in our second year, I would spend most of the week helping teachers outside Aswan. Since Sadat had ordered for largely political reasons that English should now be the top priority in schools, many non-specialists (Geography or History teachers) were abruptly required to teach the subject. Many of them could barely even speak English. Obviously, there was a useful 'multiplier effect' if we could get at these staff and give them some tuition and one or two strategies in Teaching English as a Foreign Language. Heaven knows, I was not an experienced teacher and the idea of my turning up and trying to advise mature professionals is mind-boggling, but I was young and it felt like the most sensible course of action. I blush to think of the line I took with some of the local schools inspectors, with whom I was meant to liaise, always complaining about primitive work methods and the inadequate text books. I remember asserting once, for example, that an English speaker would NEVER use the expression 'at Aswan', that the correct usage was 'in Aswan'... and a kindly inspector (the spitting image of Hermann Hesse) quietly suggested that I was being a little too dogmatic. He was right. What did I know?

In the Faiyum, there was also a showdown with the British Council, who had been a millstone round our necks since someone had decided the two organisations should work in tandem. Thus, for example, every letter that VSO sent out had to be rubber stamped by the Council, and our delightful high-minded Field Officer had to work hand in hand with a middle-aged representative who was unsympathetic to our ideals and clearly uncomfortable about the entire operation. Volunteers were a fairly disrespectful bunch, more akin to students than professionals, and almost made a point of alienating the elite expats, whom we scorned even more than tourists, though on whom we were perfectly prepared to sponge. Once when we had all been invited to an ambassadorial do, we were politely requested to wait until the Man Himself had arrived before tucking in to the feast. 'Sod the Ambassador!' was one VSO's response, and we dug in. It was all about idealism. Perhaps this is why VSO decided to start recruiting rather more mature volunteers.

Because we were so busy with our conference, we saw very little of the 'pseudo-oasis' itself, although I do remember the approach – speeding away from the fertile strip out into the desert, the Pyramids visible behind us, and gradually a glimmering emerald mirage, a vision of magical green looming up out of the tawny wilderness. It was like a sea-crossing to a haunted island, or a transformation scene from a Victorian theatre. If I were staging a production of *The Tempest* I would set it in such a desert oasis where it would need little suspension of disbelief to accept that visions might be mistaken for reality. The opening shipwreck would have to involve camels, of course, and King Alonso would need to be a sheikh, but the notion of Ariel hanging from a palm tree and Caliban heaving a water wheel is appealing. Miranda, too, would become a more believable creation in such a place, where a marriageable young girl would naturally be kept well out of sight. And Prospero drowning his books would carry a particular resonance as he stood over a well or a drainage ditch.

The Faiyum is a remnant of the original crocodile-infested Lake Moeris, whose marshy waters even now dominate the northwest corner, though the lake has shrunk to a sixth of the size it was when Herodotus and Strabo saw it. The name comes from the hieroglyphic term for 'sea': *Pa-yom*. The Faiyum was a vital granary for Ancient Egypt and a popular hunting ground for pharaohs such as Amenophis II and III, but as the lake retreated it required greater efforts to maintain. The oasis is famous for many things, such as pottery and papyri, but it is above all an irrigation engineer's paradise and has been since the Twelfth Dynasty, when it was known as The Land of the Lake (*Ta-She*) and the chief town – which later became the rather wonderful *Crocodilopolis* – was known as The Separate One (*Shedet*). There are extensive networks of drainage channels, ranks of *sakkiya* water wheels; everything is positively luxuriant, teeming with vegetation, giving visitors the impression that they are living in a green bubble, an enormous botanical garden or Egyptian Eden Project. We did briefly visit a perfume factory where the boss's son, an effete young soul, proudly showed us the family business – 'flowerth, pretht to an ethenth' – and indeed there are flowers and fruit trees stretching out to the horizon, the fields bursting with colour and life. Ironically, if people have heard of the Faiyum at all it is because of its tomb-paintings, which are not to be found on walls but on panels of cypress attached to mummy cases: 'Faiyumic portraits' from the early Christian era in a new naturalistic style, using watercolours, unbelievably lifelike. There is a poignancy to these pictures and, for us, to the oasis they were taken from. The volunteer I most associate with the Faiyum was a warm-hearted, flamboyant character, loved by everybody, with an infectious sense of humour. He adored the area and I remember him making it sound so alluring. Martin had come back safely with us from our fateful journey to Abu Simbel, but he would be the first of our band to cross that 'bourn from which no traveller returns.'

It may sound sentimental, but as time passes and we hear more and more sad news about friends from thirty years ago, I have come to realise that people were our most dependable Egyptian oasis. I hope that we were theirs. Not only the volunteers themselves and our friends and family who visited us, but those unexpected callers, some of them travellers we were able to help out and offer sustenance, some of them local people curious to meet us. I am not a naturally sociable person, but living in Upper Egypt forced me to be and it was salutary. Very often there would be Jane's home-made fudge and fresh lemon juice. Sometimes there would be poetry readings. We would sing. I would set the cassette player recording to send the tape home so that our families could hear typical Egyptian life, such as this Pinteresque scene after our return from Abu Simbel, during which several familiar cast members appear, including (we think) our Russian friend Ira, who joins in the laughter but does not speak – culturally conditioned perhaps to be wary of secret microphones:

Doorbell

AHMED 1: Sabah'el kheir [Good day] Mr John, Mrs Jane
JANE: *Ei da*? [What's that?] What a surprise... (*rustling, clinking*)
JOHN: A teapot and teacups? (*Laughter. Feet running
  downstairs.*) Ahmed's coming?
AHMED 1: Lissa.
JANE (*sotto voce*) We must hide that or he'll eat it. (*High-pitched
  Russian laughter*)
JOHN (*lid lifted*) Is this tea? Very civilised...

AHMED 2: (*Off*) Ahh...

JANE: *Hanneyan*! [Cheers] Who are the other people?

JOHN: Dunno – must be bringing a friend...

JANE: *Meen gey tany*? [Who else is coming?] (*Clinking*)

AHMED1: Ustaz Ahmed.

JANE. *Bas*? [Only?]

AHMED 1: Bas.

JANE: *Ar-bar* cups? [Four cups?]

GAMAL: Hoa owsa temanya [He wants eight] (*High-pitched Russian laughter*)

JOHN: What is this? *Ei da*? (*Arabic & laughter & rustling*)

JANE: *Ya salaam*! [My word!] (Door squeaks) *Ahlan wa Sáhlan*! [Welcome!]

JOHN: This is nice.

JANE: What is all this?

AHMED 2: For your coming! We happy for your coming! (*Laughter & thanks*)

JANE: *T'fadal* [Please...]

AHMED 1: Ezzay hal? [How are you]

AHMED 2: T'fadali...

JOHN: Take a seat.

JANE: Gracious! (*Rustling*) Beautiful.

AHMED 2: I was prepare and you prepare.

JANE: We haven't even paid you any rent yet! (*Chinking*) How superb! Milk, too!

JOHN: Teacups!

JANE: Real milk?

AHMED 2: Tea, sugar, milk...

JOHN: It's like England...

AHMED 2: In England they like this in afternoons...

JOHN: Any time...

AHMED 2: Okay? You can begin now!

JANE: You want milk in yours? Can you drink tea, Mr Gamal?

AHMED2: He shall say no but he mean yes.

JOHN: He says he can't because he is ill.

AHMED 2: Drinking with milk?

GAMAL: (*quickly*) La, mish bi'la'ban. [No, not with milk] La, m'shrab shai bi'la'ban. [No, I can't drink tea with milk]

JANE: Up to you.

AHMED 1: Ta'alah! [Come on!]

JOHN: You can't have the *bassboussa* unless you have the tea.

JANE: You want milk?

AHMED 2: Yes, okay.

JANE: Milk only or milk with tea?

JOHN: You want an ash-tray?

AHMED 1: Yes.

JOHN: Splendid.

JANE: Tea?

AHMED 2: Oh thank you.

JOHN: Don't mention it.

AHMED 2: Hamdilallah for your good coming.

JANE: About three sugars?

JOHN: Yes, we're happy to be back.

JANE: Yes, very happy to be alive.

AHMED 1 & 2: Hamdilallah.

JANE: *Hamdilallah.*

GAMAL: It is now became a memory.

AHMED1: You know, this not dangerous lake, er...

JANE: Is it not?

GAMAL: Not like big sea.

JOHN: It was very like the big sea, actually. (*Much laughter*)

AHMED2: You put sugar?

JANE: Yes...

AHMED 2: Two?

JANE: Three. *Ketir?* [A lot?]

AHMED 2: Ketir. Helwa di. [That's lovely]

So we offered the services of our water-hole and other friends did the same for us. There were certain retreats that became especially welcome as the summer came on, when supplies would dwindle in the market (no oranges or bananas, little green veg of any kind) and the sun was like a three bar electric fire in front of the face. On such days, the palm trees of the German Mission Hospital would beckon, and the thought of an eighteen-inch slice of watermelon amid the cool, green, wooden colonial style buildings where Dieter and Margaret and their children lived. The children were born in the hospital, where there was a Friesian midwife and a Finnish nurse. We saw a lot of the German couple, who spoke faultless English and fluent Arabic, though there was the curious occasion when Dieter suddenly looked at me and declared with ominous intensity: 'I think you are developing hepatitis.' In fact we had had our gamma globulin jabs at his very hospital – Stuart enduring the gaze of several giggling Nubian women as he dropped his trousers. I felt fine, I assured him; but within the week he himself had gone down with it. Dieter was an enthusiast for homeopathy and there were long conversations about dilute poisons and stool-types; my letters home show that I had become a real homeopathy crank. Then there was the luscious garden of Gerd Kloewer, whom we befriended late on in our stay. He was a Volunteer Economics Advisor to an Egyptian co-operative and lived in the old Russian consulate. He would serve us (on a small brass-bound sea chest) vanilla and lotus tea with German reconstituted synthetic cream and packet-mix *Kuchen* and offered us the use of his garden whenever we felt like it.

Certain restaurants, certain clubs were seductive too. We headed for the shade, for the spots where there would be fewest tourists or the least chance of pestering wallads. Of the local restaurants, the one we returned to most was the *Mattam el Medina*, with its shared waterglass and make-do crockery, where you could enjoy the best *ful medemmes* (beans with oil and lemon with some hard-boiled egg), or *kufta* (meat-balls) or *ta'jan* (a pot of stew) and perhaps even indulge in a puff on one of the water pipes (*sheeshas*) if you were prepared to risk lip ulcers and had a craving for hasheesh. One more upmarket favourite was beside the Old Cataract Hotel in the Feriel Gardens, overlooking the First Cataract: quite a trek from our flat at the other end of town, but worth the effort for the view and the irresistible fruit juices. There was the five-star Oberoi, too, like an airport control tower over on Elephantine Island. A certain guilt came with any trip to the Oberoi as its very existence seemed a betrayal of our VSO values and vows. But the fact that the hotel had a little bookshop quickly persuaded me. I can't remember any of the meals, I can barely recall the belly dancer, but I still have *The Book of the Dead* I bought there, all 700 pages of it. The boatman who took us

154

across (was it Charon?) was a friendly sort and told us how he sometimes transported tourists on his felucca all the way to Luxor (for LE100), but also revealed how he actually disapproved of the Oberoi. The people of Elephantine Island had been promised compensation, he said, but none came. Now the Nubian mud-brick huts jostle up against the walls of the hotel.

The West Bank was the place we took ourselves off to most frequently if we really wanted to get away from it all. Generally the Nubian villagers on that side of the Nile would leave us be and there were moments of delicious calm. But there were also the islands beyond the popular Elephantine and Kitchener, up towards the dams, some of them remnants of the old First Cataract. The few occasions we managed to swim were precious: there was something primeval about plunging in among rocks where there were hieroglyphic inscriptions, one of them allegedly referring to Biblical Joseph. We were told that Nubian villagers traditionally dipped their newborn babies in the Nile, a baptismal act that easily predates the Christian custom. Meanwhile, we would be floating among the Spinus Christi thorn bushes (once on an Easter Sunday), peering down at truly enormous catfish who showed an unhealthy interest in our toes. Ira took us visiting these islands once or twice when she was on botanical missions, and even beyond the High Dam into some of the *khiors* or fjords. There were impressive birds around, too: eagles, storks and cranes, a pelican and all the little ones I could never identify. I am no ornithologist, but our friend Dave Clow came once with his binoculars and was most excited when he spotted a golden oriole. I tried to conjure all this in 'Of Paradise' from a sequence of bird poems which Mick Imlah printed week by week in the *TLS* in the late '90s and which came to roost finally in my Horus-covered *Nightflights*:

An oriole on the islands of the First Cataract.
An osprey in the Nile as I cross on a felucca.
The egrets, white shadows of the sacred ibis.
The hoopoes, exotic moths of the midday flame.

And on the West Bank where the dead make nests
and the Nubians have been made to live in dovecotes,
a bird-catcher from one of the Nobles' Tombs
crouches with his long net, to dam the skies.

155

If such places were most precious to me because of their natural, sun-baked, open-air tranquillity, for a contained man-made scallop shell of quiet, nothing could compete with the mosque. In Upper Egypt, every city seemed to have a big new twin-towered mosque and to us they all looked alike. We came to call them 'airfix mosques' after those white plastic model-kits familiar to boys of my generation, but the most ancient of the four hundred or so in Cairo are in a different class. They vary enormously in style, from Sultan Hassan's (1356-63), reputedly built from stones from the Great Pyramid, to the Al-Nasr Mohammed Ali (1318-35), the Salih Tala'i (1160), the much restored university mosque of al-Azhar (971) to, above all, that of Ibn Tulun (876-9) the oldest and largest in Cairo. This mosque was one of the places we visited in our first few hot, bewildered, frustrated days in Egypt and it did indeed come upon us like a haven of calm in what was – even thirty years ago – a mind-numbingly busy city. The brick-built Mosque of Ibn Tulun is in a poor part of town, which makes discovering its inner glory all the more surprising. Nor is it a work of bombast, having nothing of the Mameluke extravagance, none of the audacity of the celebrated Sultan Hassan Mosque, for example, breathtaking though that is. The only 'showy' element is the helter-skelter-shaped minaret, a Moorish stone structure, climbing whose dizzying, rail-less spiral had a less than calming effect on us, though the views out towards the desert and the Pyramids were in the end restorative. To see a functioning building of this age is rare: it was erected long before anyone dreamt of cathedrals in England. What made it my archetypal oasis was the simplicity of its *sahn* or courtyard with the single domed fountain, the elegance of the surrounding layers of arches and their latticed windows, which create the kind of tranquil harmony you find in cloisters or in certain Oxford colleges, light dappling the interior arcades.

Next

They have supported him
the bronze columns

from Macedonia
to the Delta

they have sweated
and sworn

sung their coarsest Greek
across the canals

and scrub
to the Lake of Mareotis

Relaxing now
before the march
to the oasis

where Amon-Ra
will proclaim him god

Across
a fierce and wasting
white and chronic place

unclose your eyes
for an instant there

everything has shifted
shape scaled off

dune
sun
blue

hallucination

Nothing beyond the ridge
they say
We climbed it

Stretching out now
letting the northwest wind
cool them

flap their tunics dry
scour their tongues

Fishermen...
Some island...

Alexander
staring at his own
reflection
in the lake,

sees
profound wrinkles

Dinocrates of Rhodos!
he calls

And the wind
whips
as they climb
the limestone ridge

waves

that flash like convex glass
that unroll like lengths of papyrus

LETTER

Alexandria
June 1981

Dear All

I hope by now you've received the telex or I've got through to you on the phone (not the easiest of tasks, as you know) and you'll have heard that I've won First Prize at the Alexandria Poetry Festival. The prizegiving on 30th is going to be quite an event and Jehan Sadat, we think, will be presenting the prizes. Maybe the President himself will turn up. There will be TV and radio coverage and I have been asked to recite to the assembled two hundred and fifty dignitaries at sunset on the site of one of the original Seven Wonders of the World, the Pharos. Of course, we're both delighted and very excited, although sad that we can't come home as planned. Quite by chance back in the Spring I had seen the competition advertised in the Egyptian Gazette, the English language paper here:

Alex. to hold May poetry festival

THE Governor of Alexandria, Dr. Naim Abu Taleb, has decided to commemorate the cultural glories of ancient Alexandria by holding a poetry festival in May every year....
The contest will be open to all Egyptian and foreign poets.

I submitted most of the poems I had written. I shall be reading 'The Crack' and 'Tuthmosis III'. The British Council has given us a small grant to live off until the ceremony.

We've at last escaped the intolerable summer heat of Cairo (the north is so humid by comparison with Aswan) and are now in Alexandria itself where we've got to know the British Council man, and his lovely Somali wife. With his help we've been able to earn a bit of extra cash doing

161

invigilation jobs in a local French school and typing up teaching materials for the English Teaching Centre. In fact, we were paid the equivalent of two weeks' Aswan teaching for five and a half hours' work, so we can't complain. Nor can we complain about our accommodation. We've been put up in the vast house of the festival organiser, an amazing polymath who has travelled Africa in various capacities (he walked across Ethiopia), is a composer and was a racing driver. There's an armed guard outside his house because American diplomats are vulnerable. Inside, it's a home of pharaonic proportions. We have been given a guest suite – lavishly decorated with African mats, lamps and exotic furniture. There are wide gold-curtained windows, bamboo beds with patchwork quilts, and we have a maid and cook at our disposal. Most tempting to me here, apart from the electric typewriter in our room, are the three giant telescopes. Oh yes, he's an astronomer too and has a comet named after him. He gets very irritated by the constant light pollution and talks of taking an air-rifle to pop out some of the more irritating lamps nearby. He took me up on the roof last night and I saw Jupiter and Saturn magnified a thousand times through his twelve inch reflector: clear as clear, the bands round Jupiter's surface and the rings of Saturn. The moon, too, its craters unbelievably vivid. The device has a motor attached to counteract the effect of the earth's rotation, which puts things in perspective.

Alexandria itself has a melancholy beauty and I think Jane is feeling inexplicably depressed by it. I know what she means. It doesn't help when we're caught off-guard by unfortunate events like the American we were with the other night who had eaten sea urchin and abruptly developed acute food poisoning. We hammered on the door of a flat we had been told belonged to a doctor, but found only a brain surgeon who nevertheless drove the poor chap to hospital. But really we should be in celebratory mood. I've even just been out to buy some new green trousers ready for the prize-giving. But in Alexandria everything has an edge-of-the world, past-its-sell-by-date valedictory quality, everything seems to point to a pointlessness. For all the sea air, it is full of sad stories, examples of frustrated love (Constantin Cavafy, E.M. Forster) or doomed affairs (Antony, Cleopatra, Caesar). Even Lawrence Durrell couldn't filter out the city's tragic music from his surface glitter. The ghost of the celebrated Alexandria library, 'accidentally' destroyed during Caesar's campaign could be to blame: it never goes away, the thought of

900,000 scrolls, all those texts that we have never read, more Aeschylus perhaps, the earliest Homer... The mood is typified by Pompey's Pillar, one of the few antiquities remaining in Alexandria (it's believed many lie under the sea) and which stands sadly and futilely alone very near to where the library is thought to have been: some sphinxes and a few other melancholy stumps mark the spot. The pillar is made of Aswan granite and is nearly ninety feet tall. The story goes that the Prince of Savoy had twenty-two people to lunch on its capital in 1832. We have not made it yet to the famous catacombs and given the mood that the city casts on us perhaps that's wise. The other evening we wandered across the tramlines that run along the sea-front – that famously long, curving corniche – and watched the sun going down, the beach crowded with thousands of holidaying Egyptians. It seems a fitting place to be spending our final weeks.

Cleopatra at the Western Harbour

there will be
some things unchanged

the horizon
the clear skies
the deep clear ocean

and still this will break
into spasms
of opaque platitude

on the shores
around the thighs of lovers

and at their ankles
the same dismal weed
will breathe

you could also slip
and be pounded
on that pocked outcrop

there will be
some things unchanged

like the men
who haul their nets
up on the rocks there
disentangling
unconcerned by the harry
of the sea
and the seabirds

or that Caesar and I
are hurrying the waves on

I think
they will be still here
when we
are
our statues

rough protrusions

vague immaterial seabirds

they will still be here
there will be
some things unchanged

Labyrinths

I don't quite know why we didn't visit the catacombs in Alexandria, but perhaps we'd had enough of labyrinths by then and our memory of the Serapeum at Saqqara was fresh in our minds. We had been driven there, as I described earlier, by our friends from the British Council, the librarian Dave Clow and his wife Pamela. Pamela was insistent that she did not want to go in and her tone suggested that there was something about it she really did not like. The atmosphere of the site was unsettling, made more so by the refreshment area, a canopy or open tent erected in the desert where between the chairs and tables – I can see them now – half a dozen or more pye-dogs loped, jackals, living manifestations of the god Anubis. Their sinister, purposeful stride (so different from any domestic dog's) and their fearless gaze were enough to wipe out any confidence we had about descending into the Apis galleries. Had we read at the time what the French Egyptologist François Mariette put up with when he excavated here, we might have decided definitively against. His house, which is still standing near the site, was infested with snakes, scorpions, spider's webs, bats, and he describes how he cowered beneath a mosquito net while outside 'jackals, hyenas and wolves' howled at his window. Nobody interfered with those same creatures or tried to drive them away as we sat and drank our hot sweet tea. Their prowling presence was accepted as pigeons are at Paddington Station. But pigeons don't carry rabies. Nor do they evoke the god of death. Another strange presence was the nearby semi-circle of ruined statues depicting Greek poets and philosophers – Homer, Plato, Pindar – who seemed to be watching everything with cold command as if they held the end of the thread that we were about to take into the labyrinth.

The Serapeum is a series of burial chambers which were once part of a large complex of buildings dedicated to the bull god, Apis. Mariette, who knew of its existence from descriptions in classical texts, rediscovered it by chance in 1851. He had read that there was an avenue of sphinxes leading to the mausoleum and one day he spotted a stone head poking out of the sand, then an inscription mentioning Apis-Osiris. Four years later, he uncovered the entrance: 'the last finger mark of the Egyptian who set the last stone in the wall built up to cover the door was still visible in the mortar,' he wrote. 'Bare feet had left their traces on the sand strewn in a corner of this chamber of the dead'. One recent guidebook describes the experience of threading the galleries as both macabre and repulsive. It's certainly no surprise to learn that Serapis (whose name is a combination of Osiris and Apis) was the god of dreams. The chief impression I remember on entering was of an intense oppressive darkness, which seemed untouched by those few weak lightbulbs that were actually working. Having descended the ramp, ahead of us was a total blank so we had to feel our way forwards, knowing that somewhere within these fetid passageways were huge sarcophagi containing the mummified carcasses of sacred bulls. If anything, it conjured the myth of Theseus and the Minotaur, but the story as told by Herodotus is that 'the Apis-calf' came from a cow blessed by the gods in a flash of light. It would have been black with a white diamond on its brow, the sign of an eagle on its back and a scarab under its tongue. It was worshipped as the incarnation of the god Ptah, then on death 'Osirified'.

As our eyes adjusted, the sarcophagi began to loom, one after another, each filling a side vault, each a huge, single block of solid granite, black chiefly (though one or two were pink Aswan granite) and highly polished, weighing about sixty-five tons. The oldest of the bull mummies unearthed by Mariette dates back to Akhenaten's father, Amenophis III, though the ones on display were chiefly late, from the period of Ptolemy. None of this really penetrated my befuddled consciousness as we wound through the galleries. Rather, there was such a stifling atmosphere that we were increasingly keen to escape from the blackness in which this more intense blackness of black bulls within black tombs had been perpetuated. But on the way out we met one of those sights that send the modern Westerner spinning back to his namesakes. Through the gloom, we saw a granite sarcophagus lying abandoned in the very passageway we were walking down. In fact, it was only possible to get any further by squeezing between the gigantic skewed block and the passage wall. Peering inside, we saw it was empty. And a few yards further along lay its great granite lid, as if hurled down in a rage. What had happened? The temple workmen had been in the process of dragging the latest sarcophagus into place, we assumed, trying to ease it round a corner, sweat rolling off them, shouting and cursing at each other, while the priest twitted and snapped that they should show some respect, when someone called down from the entrance: *it's all over, lads, don't bother, the project's been cancelled...* The cult came to an end, the men were paid off and – as would be the case today, no doubt

– nobody was prepared to take responsibility for the clear-up, so there the sarcophagus remains.

Our experience of the Serapeum with Dave and Pamela might provide one metaphor for the process of writing this memoir: a slightly unnerving plunge into my distant past, my eyes gradually adjusting again, the shapes rising up. In the writing I have discovered what is lodged like that granite bull-coffin forever, and what has blown away. Perhaps a better, brighter, analogy would be with the recent exploration and partial raising of the city of Alexandria from beneath the sea. Excavation of a kind, in any case, is the metaphor of choice. It recurred in a poem I wrote a decade ago when we suddenly re-established contact with one of the most fascinating friends we made during our stay. Cathy dropped into our routine in Aswan (how or why I can't remember) and proceeded to enthral us with the fugal songlines her astonishing life had followed. An Oxford graduate, daughter of the author of a controversial book of theology, she knew everything there was to know about classical literature, and was – still is – altogether terrifyingly intelligent. Yet we got on so well, she was such a sympathetic and incisive woman who knew that to enjoy life to the full you had to grasp hold of the Apis horns.

Many of the visitors we met by chance and made friends with were in search of something that they couldn't quite identify, following an invisible, seductive scent that had led them moth-like to Aswan. Sometimes they had been in the country just long enough for the tap-water to start upsetting their system and they would have gone down with the dreaded 'gyppy tummy'. We became a healing no man's land, a Sekhet-Aru, where travellers could rest, take celestial food, then travel on to the great lake... Friendships made in Egypt were consequently intense and often enduring. Yet knowing, as Robert Frost put it, how 'way leads on to way', there are many people we have lost touch with since those days. I have sometimes encountered them in memory with surprise and a mournful awareness of inescapable, encroaching dark (Where is Tanzanian Jane, who had been a volunteer in the land of my Jane's lost childhood? Or the poet Martin who introduced us to the grandson of Laurence Binyon, author of 'For the Fallen'? Who were those two actors who visited us? That ex-GI who was convinced the whole place was 'gonna blow'? Austin, who lived in a Hebridean lighthouse?) But also they have risen up like statues from drowned Alexandria, friendships that we will always return to: Miles, for example, who had played the lead in *Schumann*, my first stage play, though he was and still is a Bowie fan. As he walked into our flat (three days late after being stranded incommunicado at Cairo airport) the handle of his suitcase dropped off. With Miles we walked to St Simeon's Monastery, saw an osprey on the way, and heard him mutter calmly as only a good actor could 'Oh, a snake' when he almost trod on a *tresha*. Or Debbie and Ian, whom we bumped into outside Aswan station and who were going round the world after she had lost her parents. We see them quite often: they have built one house with their own hands and are at work on another. So it continues. An old civilization is bit by bit raised from the sea, a temple is salvaged from the Nile, things are pieced back together and life goes on. While I have been reading and writing and teaching my way through thirty years, a new eight-million-book Alexandrian library has opened (Bibliotheca Alexandrina), oases have been created in the New Valley, and liberation has been dreamt of in Liberation Square.

When we arrived back in England and to the news from Hampton that Jane's mother had committed suicide before Jane could see her again, it was as if we had been set right in the middle of a new labyrinth. Our heads spun. Which way was forward? How could we know? The many dead ends were marked 'What if you had', the many circular routes were marked 'There's no point in'. *Now get yourself out of that one*, the voice came. *You have thirty years.* Keeping hold of Jane with the one hand, I clung to the thread I picked up at university, and kept following it. Pisces was led by Taurus and we left the middle, abandoned the centre, set off against the flow, and headed away from Hampton Court, our Flight out of Egypt, determined not to make money but to survive, to help others survive, and to find enlightenment. We found Vietnamese refugees to help, to guide through their own bewilderment. As we worked, new possibilities became visible, new lines that we could follow away from the roaring, the bellowing of fate, and we survived. The route that circumstances have contrived for us since 1981, though, grew up mainly out of necessity, hedged around with mortgage payments and responsibilities. The labyrinth of work and home-making and child-rearing. Having taken us north to Arbroath, it led south again to Huntingdonshire, then to New Jersey, briefly it took me to Iceland, regularly to Cornwall, and soon perhaps it will send us to Africa again. It is made of closely woven lines. The route it follows is set within the labyrinth of the ear.

Invocation

Grand mirror canal –
lead me out of this
black granite shrine

where I am becalmed in
a slave ship, eclipsed
in a solar boat. Take me

from reliefs, posturing
officials, dignitaries
with their clique language

and inflexible stance,
men with heads of beasts
that know only darkness...

The sun invites. It is
a cat's long stretched
back that leads my touch

by electricity
of night vision
down its eighth life

through hypostyle hall
to vestibule
to court

where the hawk, turning
a blind eye, believes in
himself and is unruffled.

Afterword: *Westerners*

For a poet, the first book is very special. Finding someone to publish it is the tricky part and looking back through some of the correspondence with editors from those years, it's clear I was growing very frustrated and increasingly impatient. I had obviously barked back at one small press, because I have a letter from an editor telling me how indignant she felt about my remarks but at the same time sympathising with the difficulties for any fledgling poet. It is hard to convey how it feels to be a poet but without tangible proof of the fact. In 1982 there was no alternative to the slim volume apart from the stapled, cyclostyled, self-produced pamphlet. There was no internet to post on. I was bookless in Giza, or in Arbroath, at any rate. Nor did Greening the poet have as much to offer on his CV as some: no Gregory Award, for example, although twice I had poems selected for the winners' anthology (something that still rankles though for ten years I've been one of the judges). I had not built up much of a track record with magazine publishing, except a few glorious appearances in Emma Tennant's *Bananas* – a tabloid newspaper style publication which regularly featured Ted Hughes, Peter Redgrove, Penelope Shuttle – and the various pieces Roger Garfitt had negotiated with my father's help for *Poetry Review*, which was just emerging from one of its periodic bouts of turmoil. The Alexandria Poetry Prize must have helped: it certainly sounded prestigious, yet I wonder how many people actually went in for that prize. I was told about two hundred, but I have a feeling they were chiefly poems in Arabic, so perhaps the English entrants consisted of the second-prize winner and me. There had been a couple of appearances on the BBC I could use to impress publishers, however, the first on the excellent *Poetry Now* where poets read their own work. I can't recall which poem I read or who presented it (probably Roger Garfitt) although I may have a cassette of the broadcast buried somewhere. The only script I can find is of a post-*Westerners* broadcast of one of my Tutankhamun poems when I was on the same programme as the late Michael Donaghy, who read his now celebrated poem about Alexandria ('Cadenza').

The other BBC appearance was a non-appearance. When news of my prize was broken, the World Service wanted to interview me, which for obscure reasons involved a manic desert drive to some location where a hyperactive journalist quizzed me, clearly out of his comfort zone with poetry and choosing to take rather a political line. I recited a couple of poems, including 'Westerners' and the interview was set to be broadcast months later when we were living in Scotland. In fact, it was due to go out just as we were making a long car journey, so we pulled up by the side of a Highlands road at the given time to tune in to shortwave or longwave... Nothing. And as far as I know it was never broadcast. The only explanation I was given was that the Arabic Service might have objected to something in it. What had I said? How had I offended? I wish I knew, though I have a shrewd suspicion. I am a political non-starter by comparison with a poet such as Sean O'Brien (who was also on that *Poetry Now*), but there is some charged social satire in *Westerners* and it is quite savage towards certain aspects of Egyptian life. I wonder now whether Shafik Magar of the BBC Arabic Service was involved in any way, having perceived the trouble the poems might cause in diplomatic circles. He had worked in an office near Jane's when she was in the Russian Service at Bush House. When we discovered we were being sent to Egypt, he had been very encouraging. I don't think I quite realised at the time what a respected man of letters he was in the Arab world of the 1980s. One of the fullest and most perceptive reviews *Westerners* received was by Magar in the Arabic magazine *Ad-Dastour*. It took some years to get hold of a translation – nine closely handwritten pages of tortuous English – but I could not have been more honoured to have such a response from a sophisticated Egyptian reader. The only other reaction that brought me equal pleasure was that of our Nubian friend Hassan, whom I sketched once in seven lines:

beside the fan
beneath a glass of guava

Rasselas
and *Lives of the Poets*

Dr Johnson
on the desert's edge

puffing at a sheesha

Hassan was a literary enthusiast, a teacher living on the outskirts of Aswan. He seemed to be genuinely moved by the poems in the book and wrote to me to tell me so. Later, Hassan would visit us in our home in Kimbolton and I remember him looking in wonderment at the riches on display in our modest little village shop, and picking up all the fruit and vegetables to inspect them, as our greengrocer looked on uneasily.

Shafik Magar the professional reviewer was quick to notice the political content of a poem such as 'Aswan' which now has too raw a feel to it (partly because of that lower case I favoured, learnt from the Imagists), yet it does at least aim for the heart of Upper Egypt as we knew it:

half-hearted efforts

the 'peace' bazaar
Carter   Oum Kalsoum
disco-hits

all the new hotels
with their hieroglyphs
Nefertiti heads
and Rameses colossi

on the sand
in the dirt

the people have
a swimming pool
without water

cinemas
without light

their own
palace of culture
with no chairs

and portraits of their president
but no wall to hang him on

they hardly matter
now that the fiery arc
flying up from the water there
is closing in

and the east
and the west
are scorching out their differences

ochre or rust

wringing their horny fingers

Magar called his review 'Egypt as a British poet sees it' and prefaced his three page article with that line about portraits of the president (I wonder if he caught my slyly seditious play on words). He discusses how the Egyptian writer Tawfik al-Hakim became obsessed with the Isis myth, using it to express his views on society and goes on to explain how this particular young British writer had found himself in Upper Egypt during the time of the Camp David peace agreement, that we were actually in Aswan when Carter came as a guest of Sadat. He is relieved I had not had my head turned by 'the wonders of the Valley of the Kings', though apparently I had heard 'the murmur of ancient Egypt as it whispered lofty visions' and he is swift to move to what interests him most, my 'alarming view of Egypt'. He is puzzled by such anger about the country from one who simply went there to teach its children, but emphasises that my verses 'are not the meditations of a 'foreign gentleman' standing at a distance nauseated or gloating or irritated while he watches what is happening to another country, one of the backward nations'. He recognises that in following Sartre's advice and plunging headlong into the tumult, I have fallen in love with his country (he calls it my 'misfortune'), and have been allowed to see its true face unveiled. Egypt addressed me, he wrote in conclusion, and I listened.

Roland John, who published *Westerners*, remarked of this that 'Egyptian book reviews are odd' (the only other review of such thoroughness I have had was twenty years later when John Haynes wrote about *Omm Sety*). Roland had come to the dark tower of my unpublished manuscript, taken it on to his Hippopotamus Press list and I was a happy man. Roland offered some useful suggestions and was encouraging without being patronising, which is exactly what a young poet wants. Yes, there were delays and misunderstandings before the book actually appeared in early 1983 (though 1982 is the date inside it) but its elegant plain yellow dust jacket and the space around the poems,

176

the timelessly appealing aesthetic of the design, are all down to Roland. He had also very wisely suggested that I withdraw what looks now like a misconceived piece translated from *The Book of the Dead* called 'An Ancient Song'. He was generous with the space he allowed me – eighty pages is good for a first collection – but even so there wasn't room for my Akhenaten monologue, which I still regret (though I was able to restore him to the side of Nefertiti in my 2009 'Collected', *Hunts*).

Westerners arrived at a time of considerable change in our lives. We were about to head off either to Baghdad or to Huntingdonshire: I had two applications in the pipeline. The money from my Scottish Arts Council Award had run out and I had been teaching Vietnamese refugees part-time in Dundee's Lincraig Community Centre, an area with the highest murder rate in Scotland. Although we had enjoyed visits from several of our Egypt friends – one of whom chose the very coldest time, when -27 was recorded at Braemar – life on our Arbroath council estate was becoming increasingly wearisome, 'Popeye the Sailor Man' from a circulating ice-cream van was driving me half crazy. I even stormed out and confronted the driver once, telling him I loved music and how could he possibly do this to a sensitive soul like me... It turned out he was a violinist and a lovely man. More importantly, though it was almost not mentioned between us, we were moving towards starting a family. But we hung on, waiting for job interviews, while the local authority decided it would tear out all the new storage heaters it had installed on our estate the year before and replace them with a different type. We salvaged ours and it is still warming our bedroom. I remember the electrician who had to disconnect it opening the cupboard to the meter and finding a large poster of the youthful, shaven-headed Tutankhamun. 'A fine head of hair,' he muttered in a broad Angus accent.

Meanwhile, my parents were leaving their beloved London for a new life in the Peak District, in Marple with its flight of sixteen locks, which always made me think of those sixteen steps to Tutankhamun's tomb. I can't remember what they thought of my applying to Iraq (and thank Heavens we kept well out of Saddam's clutches). Before I put in for the British Council post and the teaching job at Kimbolton, I did apply for Writer in Residence at Paisley Library. This was Douglas Dunn's old stamping ground. Douglas I had got to know because he was Writer in Residence himself in Dundee at this time. He took me to lunch with Edwin Morgan on one famous occasion, who had lived in Egypt; there were jokes, I recall, about 'Copts and robbers'... I had an interview at Paisley on the eve of receiving my first copy of *Westerners*. I spent some time looking round the museum with its small selection of Egyptiana, and even chatted in the interview about how I might be able to use this material in my job, getting children interested in it... I lost out to James Kelman, author of the wonderfully titled *Not Not while the Giro*, a much better choice of candidate.

Reader, we ended up in Kimbolton and I arrived clutching a copy of the Yellow Book, which I was soon able to give to a poet I found working here, born in the same year as me. Stuart Henson's continued presence and inspiration and encouragement have been among the best reasons for staying in Huntingdonshire for thirty years, for becoming a confirmed Westerner in one sense or another. Moreover, my future Head of Department and my Director of Studies were both veterans of Sudan. What this Londoner has become is, I think, as much the gift of the Nile as the Thames, though he was born on that river's banks: 'It took/the Nile to loose the river's/world serpent grasp/on our lives' as I wrote in a long poem, 'Thames', playing with that river's own Oxford name in the last lines, though not knowing then that our young Katie would end up at New College: 'Soon I will take our daughter/so she can know the Thames,/Sweet Thames, the silent/longing and searching of Isis.' All we have in Kimbolton is the little river Kym, a dried up ditch for much of the year, though it has been known to have its own inundation and properties nearby have installed floodgates. We have been happy here in Larkin's sense that 'nothing, like something, happens anywhere'. The two Egyptian years hang like a backdrop to whatever small dramas and Pinteresque dialogues have ensued as daughters have been born, friendships have come and gone, parents have died, house prices have risen and fallen, and we remain in the little cottage we bought because it seemed unextravagant, in keeping with the spirit of what we had undertaken in our two years up the Nile.

The Amarna Stelae

At Karnak, who was it unearthed
in nineteen twenty-five
those twenty-five colossi
of Akhenaten? In the photograph
they rise up out of the sand
like science fiction clones
or giant ivory chessmen
dropped at the end of a game
on a beach in the Hebrides.

They are caricatures of what
these twenty-five years
have made of one who stood
arms folded and holding
a flail to palely control
a class of Egyptian girls.
After me. What's your name?
Mr John, Mr John,
where you get pot belly?

Too much of Egypt has gone
to try and reconstruct
determinatives. Look at this
album with half its photos
fallen out, odd inscriptions
above blurred faces; at our
spoilheap of slides and this
cine we cannot translate
into any blank cartouche.

Voices that cheered the First
Cataract with us or sang us
to Kitchener's Island have fallen
dumb, have dried at their source
to the fixed mummy-smiles
of Tjuyu and Yuya, a mother
and father, her hair plaited,
his mouth opening. My parents
have stopped singing, too.

At the Colossi on the West Bank
where we leaned our hired bikes
and Dad's *ka* went out
of control for lack of sugar
(sugar stirring all about us),
lumps of crumbling figure
guard a temple that has gone,
though a spirit free-wheeled there,
Akhenaten's gold begetter.

Was it love or self that drove us
to escape high priests and viziers,
to find a freer style for our
marriage in that bow of the Nile,
an aim fletched with the Truth
Feather, to penetrate the Window
of Appearance? Glass shimmering
between us. The Priests of Money
putting paid to the experiment.

The Hidden One proclaims
Akhenaten's move was politic,
the sun he worshipped was himself,
his Venusian features, woman's
pelvis, spindly limbs,
curved spine, bent
knees were caused by a disease
which made him blind and led
to such touching scenes of intimacy

with Nefertiti, who was never
exiled to that 'castle in the north'
but changed her name, her sex,
became co-regent, left
posterity and Hitler the face
she wished to show, turning
a blind eye as the wall
came down, and mocking
all other women.

Checkmate. The king is dead.
These stelae mark his boundaries.
We live on as minimalists
dreaming a Tutankhamun
might clear our title to a castle
or fix the roof. Our daughters
breathe the western wind –
but one has asked for a scarab
and one is a worshipper of the sun.

GLOSSARY OF COLLOQUIAL ARABIC FEATURED IN THE TEXT
(spellings will often vary during transliteration; hard g is pronounced j in Upper Egypt)

Ahlan wa sáhlan!	One of many formal expressions of welcome
ei da?	What's that?
aiwa	Yes
Allah!	God, but – as in English – also expression of surprise
Allahu Akbar	God is great
ána	Me
baksheesh	A tip, or small change: alms
balladi	Brown unleavened bread, but it means local or native
bassboussa	Sweet and sticky cake
bersim	Clover fed to animals
betekállem arabi?	You speak Arabic?
bismillah	In God's name
bi-surrah	Oranges 'with a navel' – the best kind
bowab	A porter
bukra	Tomorrow (or some point in the future)
doum	Fruit of the doum palm
ensha'allah	God willing (accompanies any mention of the future)
etfaddal	Please take – the equivalent of 'bitte' in German
ezzay hal?	How are you?
fain?	Where?
fellahin	Rural working men, 'peasants'
fino	White loaves
ful	Cooked fava beans, a staple food
gallabiya	Loose fitting garment worn by men
hamdillallah!	Thank God
hanneyan	Wishing someone good fortune, 'cheers!'
hantour	Horse-drawn carriage
haram	Shame
hawagga	A tourist, a foreigner
helwa	Lovely
ideeni	Give me

karkodeh	Hibiscus flower drink
ketir	Many
kufta	Meatballs
kwai'yes	Good
la'ban	Milk
lissa	Not yet
mabruk	Congratulations
madra'sa	School
maleesh	Never mind
modaris	Teacher
maquaggi	A dhobi or professional ironer
milayeh	Dark outer garment worn by women
mulukhia	Slimy but popular vegetable dish
Nasrani	A Christian (i.e. linked with Nazareth)
Nubee	Nubians
'otta	Cat
'oud	A kind of lute
'ows?	want it/one?
rababa	A two-stringed fiddle or bowed lyre
Rub el Khali	The Empty Quarter
sabah'el kheir	Good day
Sa'idi	Upper Egyptian
Saad-el-Aali	The High Dam
sakkiya	Water wheel
shaduf	See-sawing device for raising water
shai	Tea
shamsi	Sun-baked bread
sheesha	Hubble-bubble (water-pipe)
souk	Market
ta'jan	Stew
tamarahindi	Tamarind drink
tresha	Viper or asp
ustaz	Mr or Sir
wadi	Valley
wahida wahida	Slow down, take care, one step at a time
wallad	Boy
ya salaam	Good heavens!

Acknowledgements

I am very grateful to Meirion Jordan of Gatehouse for his initial interest in this memoir and to both him and Sam Ruddock for their attention to detail in the editing. I appreciated too their readiness to include my daughter's drawings, which it moves me greatly to see alongside my work. Thank you, Rosie.

Thanks to the publishers of the following books in which poems have appeared: *Westerners* (Hippopotamus Press, 1982), *The Tutankhamun Variations* (Bloodaxe, 1991), *Nightflights* (Rockingham Press, 1998), *Omm Sety* (Shoestring Press, 2001), *Hunts: Poems 1979-2009* (Greenwich Exchange, 2009).

Some of the poems were originally published in *Argo*, *Encounter*, *The Egyptian Bulletin*, *The Gregory Awards Anthology 1981/2*, *Gregory Poems 1983-84*, *Orbit* (VSO), *Poetry Review*, *Quadrant* (Australia), *The Review* (Canada), *Swansea Review*, *Times Literary Supplement*, *The World & I* (USA). Copyright remains with the author.

Many thanks to all our Egyptian *asháb* (friends), many of whom are recalled in these pages, to family and friends who visited us or wished they could, and to those volunteers who were out with us 1979-81.

I owe perhaps the biggest debt of gratitude to VSO for accepting Jane and me in the first place and then deciding not to send us to Papua New Guinea.

List of Images by Rosie Greening

Biographical Note

John Greening lived in Aswan, Upper Egypt for two years with his wife, Jane. In 1981 he won First Prize at the Alexandria International Poetry Festival and received the award from Jehan Sadat on the site of the ancient Pharos. Since then, he has published over a dozen collections, won Arvon, Bridport and *TLS* Prizes and received a Cholmondeley Award. Recent publications include his OUP edition of Edmund Blunden's *Undertones of War*, the anthology *Accompanied Voices: Poets on Composers from Thomas Tallis to Arvo Pärt*, a new selection of Geoffrey Grigson's poetry, the Egyptian pamphlet *Nebamun's Tomb*, and *Heath*, a collaboration with Penelope Shuttle. He is a regular reviewer for the *TLS*, an Arvon tutor, and a judge for the Eric Gregory Awards. He has just completed two years as RLF Writing Fellow at Newnham College, Cambridge.

Rosie Greening studied English at Exeter, and currently works as an Editor/Writer at Make Believe Ideas.

Gatehouse Press